Praise for Alexandra Roxo

"Alexandra Roxo is hell-bent on teaching women how to live life to the fullest."

Shalayne Pulia
InStyle magazine

"Simply being around Roxo's exhilarating, vivacious presence is a revitalizing retreat in and of itself."

Kara Ladd
lifestyle partnerships editor, *Harper's Bazaar*

"Juicy spirituality! The ultimate read for those ready to step into their whole damn self."

Emma Mildon
bestselling author of *The Soul Searcher's Handbook* and *Evolution of Goddess*

"Come for the meditation coaching, stay to get in touch with the divine feminine within."

Marisa Meltzer
New York Times columnist

DARE

TO

FEEL

Also by Alexandra Roxo

F*ck Like a Goddess: Heal Yourself.
Reclaim Your Voice. Stand in Your Power.

DARE TO FEEL

The
Transformational
Path of the Heart

ALEXANDRA ROXO

sounds true
BOULDER, COLORADO

Sounds True
Boulder, CO

Published 2024

Book design by Charli Barnes

Printed in Canada

BK06780

Library of Congress Cataloging-in-Publication Data

Names: Roxo, Alexandra, author.
Title: Dare to feel : the transformational path of the heart / Alexandra
    Roxo.
Description: Boulder, CO : Sounds True, [2024]
Identifiers: LCCN 2023015369 (print) | LCCN 2023015370 (ebook) | ISBN
    9781649631770 (hardcover) | ISBN 9781649631787 (ebook)
Subjects: LCSH: Self-actualization (Psychology) | Conduct
    of life.
Classification: LCC BF637.S4 R699 2024 (print) | LCC
    BF637.S4 (ebook) | DDC 158.1--dc23/eng/20230707
LC record available at https://lccn.loc.gov/2023015369
LC ebook record available at https://lccn.loc.gov/2023015370

10 9 8 7 6 5 4 3 2 1

For the deep feelers who are daring
and raw and fierce and tender,
unafraid of their shadows,
and calling forth their deepest truths,
opening their hearts again and again,
unapologetically, without shame,
and who know that this is the spiritual work.

Contents

Contents

Feeling: A Reclamation

Most of us weren't taught how to feel. In fact, I would argue that most of us were taught *not* to feel. For example, as a child, you were likely told you couldn't pee at school until it was time for break. You are six years old, and you drank your juice at lunch like you were supposed to, but now you aren't allowed to pee. You are trying to focus on 1 + 1 = 2, but your bladder is starting to burn. So, what do you do? You learn how to stop feeling. You learn how to stop listening to the sensations, signs, and signals of your body, and in learning how to ignore these, you quickly learn to override your most basic needs.

As a bonus side effect, parents and society praise you for being "good." You learn that it pays not to make a fuss. When you feel hurt that you were left out on the playground and you go cry to a teacher, you are reprimanded for complaining, or you are told to cheer up and to "not let it get to you." And so, you learn to smile through your pain. You learn to grin and bear it. Instead of playing and dreaming, you focus on getting good grades. You are proud of yourself for this warriorness; it is survival. It's not safe to feel everything you are feeling.

Even if you have the courage to ask them, most of the time the adults around you are too busy to hold you in the pain of being picked on at lunch, too busy to stop and share in your delight at spotting a giant orange butterfly dancing through the air. They, too, are concerned with survival, putting food on the table and keeping you from running into traffic. They are worried about money. They are stuck in their own shit.

When you stub your toe and are wailing on the floor in the grocery store, honoring your pain with tears and shrieks, they are embarrassed; crying like that in the grocery store is not okay. You are hushed, placated, or ignored. There is little space for your inconvenient, real-time feelings in their world. So, you take the lollipop that says, "Shhh," or you shove your thumb in your mouth and zone out watching dancing, animated fish on the TV.

And some of you experience frightening things that you don't know how to face. You freeze parts of your true self in the face of trauma, and for good reason. Terror makes you hide inside yourself. Your tiny body doesn't know how to handle or process the painful or heartbreaking or invasive experiences of abuse or neglect or abandonment, or of looking or feeling different than the others. You may be a sensitive soul, but your psyche is strong. It helps you tuck the felt memory of these experiences away into the tissue of your cells, hiding things from yourself that are too hard to digest.

By the time you're in middle school, you can hold back tears, poop, laughter, and insane menstrual cramps, and no one is the wiser. You are amazing at suppressing feelings and sensations and emotions. You rarely even need to cry, and you're proud of it! Sometimes, though, the emotions catch up with you like a tidal wave, and you feel so overwhelmed you don't know what to do. You sob in a heap on the floor and get up and try to face life again. When life gets intense and the feelings threaten to overtake you, you calm yourself by bingeing on sweets or staring numbly at the TV. Or you begin to count calories. Tallying up every Cheerio you place into your mouth becomes the perfect distraction from everything that is going on inside you. As puberty hits and the hormones rage, controlling something like food feels safe. There are likely no rites of passage to hold you. No circle of crone mamas to say, "It is safe to feel, it is safe to cry." So, you play it cool and do whatever you can to fit in.

But the truth is that not feeling hurts you. Controlling your feelings by numbing or silencing them creates a pattern inside of you that may go on your whole life. Denying your emotions and your felt sense of life is denying your reality. It creates a spiritual and psychological split from your true self. It may seem safer to deny the moving opera of your soul incarnate, but it is not. Denying and controlling your felt experience shuts down the voice of your soul, eroding the link between you and your life, you and your body, you and this world, you and the divinity that yearns to speak to you.

Fast-forward twenty years, and your innocent survival tactics have become dark and gnarly. Even if you want to feel the pain and joy in your body, you can't. The habit is too deep. Now you're in therapy learning to feel again, and it's brutal. Perhaps you feel a lot, but it comes in tidal waves of emotion that you can't control. Maybe you're engaged in a push-pull with feeling—numb the tough ones, try to enhance the good ones—and now you're a mess. You know it is time to thaw the layers of ice that have frozen the feelings in your body. To break down the walls you've built around your heart. To stop smiling through your pain. To stop eating your feelings. Or drinking or working or shopping them away. You want to start being honest with yourself and the people around you. The idea of this terrifies you, but somewhere deep inside, you know it is the only way to liberate the truth of who you are, to know yourself, to live honestly and openly.

And slowly, over time, you learn to feel in real time again. You remember how to feel the pain in your body. The grief in your heart. Your capacity for childlike wonder and delight. Feelings no longer come in waves that threaten to drown you, but they exist as an ongoing symphony that you are learning to live within. Taking time to feel "slows you down" from maximum productivity, but somehow you know you must do it. You are ready to cultivate compassion for your family, your friends, the trees and animals dying in the Amazon. You find yourself crying over the injustices in the world. And you cultivate compassion for yourself. For the things you have endured, the things you didn't know how to feel, the things that got stuck in your body and turned you tough or hard or scared. You hold the little one inside of you with so much love. You understand that feeling is the language of the Divine, the way the Mystery speaks to you and through you.

3

At first you are truly overwhelmed. It is insane to feel this much. But over time, it gets easier. You learn to be with the waves of emotions and sensations. You learn not to identify with them and instead let them wash over you like a giant, cleansing wave. You hear messages in all of it. You feel truth pulsing through you. You regain a connection to the eternal essence that you are. All this feeling *feels like being alive*. It feels like connection to yourself and life. You are more shining and open now. Your eyes glisten with tears as you stop to watch a sunset, absorb what is happening in the news, and spend evenings laughing with your loved ones. There are times when you feel you can't hack it; it's too hard. So, you rest, and then you come back to your heart. And slowly, it opens again, little by little, and even though it is terrifying, it feels amazing. You are open to life again. You are home in your body again. You did it. You dared to feel. You opened your spiritual heart. You plugged deeply into Source and learned to trust that connection again.

This quite accurately describes my own journey of reclaiming my full-feeling self, of trusting my feeling self as a language of connection to Spirit, of finding balance beyond the pendulum swing of too much feeling and not feeling at all, and walking the transformational path of the open heart. For most of my life, I either let the feelings coming from my wide-open heart drown me, or I pushed them down and muscled my way out of them. I didn't always want to hear what they had to say. This continued until one day I realized that this dysfunctional relationship with feeling was costing me my joy and presence, preventing me from receiving love, cutting me off from my spiritual journey and my body, and generally wreaking havoc on my life. I knew that unless I stopped to feel, and in turn heal, and began to listen, I would never experience the life I longed for. I would never feel the joy I yearned for. I would live in my head, cut off from the deep embodiment of my soul.

Life could fly by while I remained checked out, numbed out, frozen, and stuck in my thoughts. This reckoning with my body and soul was necessary and urgent. I also knew on some level that feeling was a way I was in contact with the Divine, and that when it was blocked, I became disconnected from my eternal nature and my spiritual path. I was stuck in the rational world, the thinking world, a world without the numinous magic of what exists beyond words in the felt senses, intuition, and instincts, and in living deeply embodied.

Animals move through life with keen senses and instincts. Healthy animals can smell a storm coming, sense danger, and shake off trauma. They instinctively roll around in playful delight. They are a part of nature, not separate from it. This connection to our own instincts is something we humans have lost. Though this book isn't a reclamation of the instinctual self per se; it is an invitation for us modern-day humans to begin to deeply feel each other and our lives again through the depth of an open heart, the "brain" of our feeling self, and in turn let that be an invitation to reclaim a sense of embodied spirituality and live from what I call the "transformational path of the heart."

This is a book about the spiritual journey of the heart's feeling and not feeling, opening and closing, numbing and withdrawing, diving deeply into the heart's shadows, healing, and finally learning to stay open. In this book I will invite you to feel the good, the bad, and the ugly, using my own heart-wrenching and heart-expanding stories of walking the transformational path of the heart to help you access the wells of feeling inside of you. These stories are about my own soul's journey, but they are yours, too. They are a part of our shared human experience and what we all feel. They will call forward memories in you that you can now recognize as your own heart's initiations, the lessons that called you into deep feeling, deep opening, deep healing, and change. They are access points to every soul's journey of human experience. They belong to everyone who has experienced loss, shame, loneliness, joy, love, and more. The feelings we experience as human beings, and the situations that give rise to them, are universal. They are what human biology and mythology are made of. Without seeing our lives in the context of the spiritual path, the soul's journey of deep learning, and the heart's journey of deep opening, life experiences can seem mundane. But they are keys to how we know love and how we honor the great Mystery that created us. It is when we dare to feel, and, in doing so, dare to open the heart, that we are available to truly feel the immensity and magic of life. In each deep dive into openhearted feeling, we say yes to being made, molded, crafted, and opened by Goddess/God/the Divine . . . by the experiences that we came to this planet for, as souls seeking awakening.

These are true stories about my own walk on the transformational path of the heart, feeling my way through core wounds, discomfort, heart opening, dark nights, and all states between. Some of the stories may be activating as I occasionally talk about things like addiction, alcohol and drug use, suicidal ideation, sexual trauma, and mental health struggles. If something is activating to you, take your time, take a breath—there is no need to rush yourself. Within our shared humanity I hope we can all sense the healing potential and feel less alone in our own struggles. Also, some of the names have been changed to protect people from my past and be respectful of where people are today. But the names of my dear friends have stayed the same.

In this book, "feelings" encompasses emotions, sensations, instincts, and intuitive hits, all of which are experienced in the body. Feeling is the language of the heart and extends to the body and soul. Feeling is a way Spirit reaches into us, speaks to us, and lives through us. Much of the canon of self-help, personal development, and modern spirituality can feel intellectual, data-driven, or how-to driven, offering instructions and advice flattened into digestible memes. There are stats on how meditation can help you become calmer and more productive. There is data showing exactly how the nervous system becomes dysregulated and how to regulate it again. There are step-by-step formulas to drive these teachings home. It is becoming increasingly common to psychologize all emotional experience and analyze emotions and feelings. This is a helpful part of all our journey of awareness and healing collectively, but it can also lead to over-processing, getting stuck in the head, and losing contact with the spiritual gifts of our felt experiences. I myself am a forever student of psychospiritual theory; I love learning with my mind, and yet I am cautious to remember that on the spiritual path there are places beyond intellectual understanding, places where the deep mystery exists in myth, story, feeling, poems, and in the well of the spiritual heart.

The aforementioned "transformational path of the heart" is the choice to experience life through the spiritual heart, to study how it opens and closes, how it recovers from hurt, how it learns to trust again, and how it dares to feel as a way of connecting to all of reality. This path is ineffable, mystical, artistic, nonlinear, and beyond reason. I worship at the temple of that which is felt in the body, the visceral, the sensual, the sensorial, and the primal as key aspects of my connection to the Divine. In my practice as a teacher, facilitator, and spiritual guide, I support people to connect with their soul, their deepest yearnings, and the divinity within through embodiment. Allowing emotions to be pathways to deep openings and pulling concepts and ideas through these bodies, feeling how the body inhabits the soul self and how the senses are an extension of the soul and our divinity. This is an opposite spiritual path to how many of us were conditioned, where we seek to calm ourselves and our senses and stay in the realm of prayer or meditation, seeing holiness as existing outside of ourselves and not as something to be found when we descend into the chaos and magic of all that is going on in the body and the soul that inhabits our tissues and emotions.

In a spiritual space that can feel oversaturated with left-brain analysis, this book is an invitation for you to get to know yourself from the perspective of the right brain, the heart, and the body; from a place of experience, feeling, and deep knowing, where meaning is *divined* rather than explained. As such, this book is an invitation into a felt experience in your body, using storytelling and poems and rituals to share spiritual truths. This is an ancient way of teaching, sharing, and transmitting wisdom that I believe is ripe for reclamation. Stories get us out of our heads and into our hearts. They teach us without making us feel like we're "learning a lesson." They take us on a journey and leave us changed. Stories are not simply for entertainment but also for catharsis, transformation, illumination, and possibility. Stories are a way we feel into our archetypal similarities and access the deeper myths that all humans experience.

As for why we need to hear each other's stories, and why it is time to dare to feel? **As we navigate lives spent more and more online, being in our bodies, in our hearts, open and revealed, human to human, breath to breath, becomes scarier, riskier, and more vulnerable.** Texting someone when something big or heavy comes up feels easier than connecting on the phone or having a coffee and chatting in person. The bubbles of fear and anxiety we feel in the face of real connection become less and less tolerable the less we practice feeling them. We unconsciously begin to skip out on in-person events or live experiences because we don't want to feel awkward, vulnerable, or exposed. Or we show up and reach for a drink or a joint to take the edge off, feeling all of this is too much for our system when we aren't used to it. Was it the pandemic? Is it technology? Does it matter? It is happening.

And slowly, we begin to shut down and isolate, spending more and more time staring into screens. We avoid taking a step closer to another person because we fear our feelings will be rejected or that we will say the wrong thing. We sidestep anything we deem "too intense," those moments of emotion or sensation that we cannot control. But in doing this, we avoid the miracles of *boundless* joy, *uncontrollable* excitement, and *overwhelming* passion. The more we try to control or retreat from feeling, the more we shrink away from some of the greatest parts of being human: crying, loving, connecting, and taking ... e, work, and creativity. All of this requires a willingness ... e present in our bodies, to OPEN, and to BREATHE. This is ... member that we are not in control. This is where we recall ... piritual path outside of any religion we were born into.

Where we leave the worship of money and productivity and fame and come into devotion to our shared journey, to the planet, to the Mystery, to something other than ourselves. **We do not simply enter the spiritual path to "feel" better. We enter to feel it *all*. We enter to know the divine. We enter to be fully embodied this lifetime and to awaken.** Feeling is a gateway to compassion and empathy, which pull us out of the experience of the self and into the greater collective experience. It takes courage to feel, but it is also a relief to stop trying to control everything and to stop feeling like we are each so different as individuals. As we feel more into our lives, we develop more empathy for the lives of others, seeing the universal experiences we are all a part of. We relax and open into our sameness.

This is when the armor begins to come down. This is when we begin to stop checking out, overthinking, fidgeting, grabbing for our phones, numbing out with substances, or running for the door. There may be tears, some awkwardness, some giggles. But when we stay ready to open up, heart to heart, body to body, there is a stillness, a gush of love, a shining jewel, a *something* that we cannot put into words. Our feelings are the messy indicators of our humanness, and this is what we miss when we spend our lives avoiding them. We must stay in the practice of feeling the real, the touch of life upon our skin, air, breath, nerves, tension, awkwardness, and all. **Feeling is a devotional act to living in the real world as opposed to existing in a flat, virtual simulation of life.**

But let it be known: daring to feel and to walk the transformational path of the heart is not for the faint of heart! It is dark and it is gritty. It is tears and blood and guts. It is flying high in the sky and descending below the earth's surface to sit in dark soul caves and listen and learn there. It is not clean and pristine; it requires you to roll up your sleeves and get your hands dirty and dare to walk in the dark. Daring to feel requires a full activation of your being, your nervous system, your sensual body, your emotions, your fears. It also requires facing your past and the traumas and experiences that taught you it was not safe to feel. It requires laying your life on the altar of heart transformation even when doing so feels terrifying.

Not only will this daring eventually unleash your joy and bliss but it will also stir up any past hurts that have been imprinted in this body that has carried you through life. For anybody who has experienced deep hurt, and whose body has been holding and hiding this hurt away for years, this can be overwhelming. As a result, as you begin to dare to feel, you will sometimes feel backed into a corner, like you want to run from the room. Logic will try to convince you that there is somebody or something out there who is better for you, who won't trigger you to look at your blind spots, your hard spots, or your pain spots. All the voices of the conditioned mind will chime in at this point with their insecurities and fears; in an attempt to keep you "safe," they will instruct you to walk away. "This is *too much* feeling, too much openness," they will say. This is a part of walking the heart path. It has been said by many a mystic that it is a warrior's path to walk with an open heart in this world.

And it is in the seeming unsafety of staying with the feelings of your open heart, and keeping it open, that you break free. In these moments, the work is to feel the kinks and knots in your heart, and to sit with them and tend to them and breathe with them. To feel your stubbornness. Your inability to open. Your fear of commitment. Your fear of seeming needy. Your avoidance masked as "self-sufficiency." And, slowly, you will begin to see them simply as waves of experience, of karma, or as remnants of past moments in your life that are coming up to be burned away on the path of your soul's liberation from fear and suffering. That which was once so hard will become simple when it is approached as your daily spiritual practice, the practice you live into your whole life: living from an open heart and accepting all of your emotions as passing moments to feel into, without pushing them away.

When we are able to move toward our feelings rather than running from them, these moments of deep feeling remind us of who we truly are. They soften us, they teach us, they open us, they reveal artful, beautiful truths. The process of opening after deep closure is different for everyone. It may require time with a trusted mentor or therapist, or attending a twelve-step meeting. Or it could be you and your journal and this book and moments of deep breathing when a wave of grief comes. There is no right or wrong way to open, and no timeline or reason to rush the process. Your deep opening to feeling and to your spiritual heart is your own journey.

As we move deeper into our honest emotional and spiritual realms, our underbellies are revealed, our fears are given a voice. It is in the delicate, vulnerable place of letting go of control that we get to observe our reactions, patterns, and closures. The reward for this risk-taking is knowing ourselves and feeling our lives more deeply. It is living with more love and less fear. It is an ability to stay loving and compassionate in more moments than not and to give others permission to do the same.

And now, we begin to recognize that this feeling is the language of *connection*, which is where the heart path lives. Connection to our bodies, ourselves, our souls, the world around us, to the Divine, and, last but not least, each other. When we stop feeling, we stop connecting authentically. We stop feeling empathy for our communities at large. We stop caring about the collective experience. Sometimes not feeling is a necessary form of self-protection, a way of surviving for little ones who don't know better. But as adults, when we inhibit feeling the tough stuff, or shy away from discomfort, we cut off our potential to feel each other. We cut off our potential to feel and give and receive love deeply. We cut off our potential to heal through some of the greatest issues on this planet, issues that derive from us experiencing each other as separate. Feeling each other makes it so much more difficult to hurt each other. If politicians felt with their hearts, would they still make decisions that hurt whole populations of people? **When we dare to feel, we cannot turn away and ignore the suffering of others.** This is where, as a human race, we are being asked to evolve into a felt understanding that war, and the pillaging of the earth, and the stealing of lands, is hurting all of us. And it all begins with feeling our own heart, our own pain, and our own joy and bliss. We cannot skip over this part of the process.

If you're reading this, you know this. If you are here, it is because you have likely already dared to feel, walking along this particular transformational path, and you have had a taste of what it means to let in both the deep pleasures and the pains of life. Perhaps you have even experienced the transformational power of engaging with the messy, complex, and wide array of sensations, feelings, and emotions that are your embodied essence.

If you're not quite there, or you're hungry for more, in this book, I'll go first. I'll show you the times when I shut down, numbed, and turned away from life, closing my heart from pain and fear; the times feeling this world overwhelmed me; the times I dared to reopen my heart; the times I dared to feel and how, in the process, my soul was crafted, and I found the Divine within me. I will invite you to feel *with me* moments that shook me to my core and ones that revealed the true self that had been there all along. These are some of my initiations along the transformational path of the heart.

Along the way, I will also share practices that have helped in my own heart's opening and spiritual journey. I have also included poems that I channeled during times of deep loving and deep grieving, and rituals to help you call forth your own deep-feeling self. I present all of this as medicine for your heart and as a gentle invitation in the direction of deep feeling, connection, and the divine flow of life. I want to give you the courage to feel the depth of your heart's expression, the array of feelings and sensations in you—to claim them as your own and to not be afraid or ashamed of them. I want to give you permission to let yourself be floored by life and to see what is being offered to you in your most openhearted moments: an opportunity to transform, grow, open, expand, and know yourself more deeply. An opportunity to let the Divine energetic flow of life move through you, unencumbered, trusting it deeply, not trying to control it. And for this act to be not just for you and your healing but to radically connect you to this planet, all of humanity, the body of the earth, the trees, and our collective human story that we are smack dab in the process of transforming, day by day.

Ultimately, this is where I want to guide you with the writings, rituals, and practices I present here. But before we dive in together, I want to remind you again that daring to feel is a revolutionary act—because feeling is the language of our shared humanity and of our spirituality. Only when we feel can we understand how others feel, can we cultivate empathy. If we all dared to feel what is happening on this planet, how could we turn away? When we see someone suffering, we can either shut the feelings down or we can turn toward that suffering, feel it, breathe it through our hearts, and allow grief, compassion, and kindness to emerge and call us into action. But this internal opening and shift can only happen when we dare to feel. We need to ask ourselves: Do we have the courage to feel the spectrum of suffering on this planet? Are we willing to allow this to propel us into compassionate action, as daunting as that may sound? This is the mark of walking the transformational path of the heart.

Feeling is also presence: staying present to our experiences. Staying present to our bodies. Staying present to each other. Feeling requires awareness and presence. A ground or bowl to hold the waters of feeling. So, in this book, not only will you have the courage to feel but also to cultivate a presence that can hold the feelings that you experience without drowning in them. Each time you reflect and sit in the contemplations I call you into, you are cultivating presence and awareness to hold the well of the waters of emotions as your spiritual practice.

There are experiences and feelings that open and shatter us and expand us past the small self, that bring us into stars and sky, into the wider human myth, if we let them. And there are emotions and experiences that bring us into the soil and blood and death portals, into roots and mud, and another place beyond this world. As we offer our hearts freely to life's ups and downs, without holding back, we practice being a part of the whole; we see where the personal is the whole, and where one story is all our stories. We turn ourselves on to all of life. Daring to live life awake! Embodied! Daring to enjoy all of life, from the agony to the ecstasy.

The fact that you are reading this book tells me that you are ready to live with an open heart, deeply embodied, and that perhaps you are no longer afraid of feeling it all and living in deep connection with the world. It tells me you are ready to see the transformational path of the heart as your teacher, your ultimate healer, and the light illuminating the pathway to your soul's liberation. At the most profound level, it tells me that you desire to experience a return to an internal state of union with the Divine and uncover the unconditional love that you are in the ground of your being, at your center, underneath the shifting tides of human experience. My hope is that these writings give you permission to weep, the freedom to open up and feel big, and the inspiration to take risks in your living and your loving as you begin to de-armor your heart and share it with the world. Above all, I want to remind you of the depth of beauty, meaning, and connection to self and others that is available to us when we commit to feeling it all, even when it hurts. And that this, too, is Divine.

YOU CHOOSE

Your Being can be
an act of Awakening.
An act of Protest.
An act of Love!

Or an act of complacency,
an act of pretending,
an act of holding it together.

Moment to moment, you get to choose.

Will your thoughts beam out from your mind and heart,
hitting people like hidden laser beams of love?

Will you lace your laughter with healing,
walking through the world
leaving a trail of light?

Will you create an invitation,
unspoken,
a hand that reaches out to all you encounter,
inviting them into a portal of Peace?

Or will you stick with:
"How are you?"
And "I'm fine."

Because it's more convenient?

You choose.

PART 1

HEARTBREAK

Learning Not to Feel

I started avoiding feeling when I was a little girl. I am not special in this avoidance. Culturally it was asked of us all. And while some may have eschewed this social imprint, many of us did not. Many of us learned to smile through all our pains and be sweet little girls and boys who did our homework, sat up straight, didn't cry in public, and learned to hold it in and be strong. I have met some people who did not get this programming. Perhaps there was safety for them as children to feel, to create security, to let their insides be revealed on the outside without dropping that connection. But many of us learned to disconnect the inner and outer worlds at a young age. "Smile," they would tell us. And we would, even though inside we were in agony.

At six years old, I was in Miami with my father, who I only saw twice a year. We were in his BMW; he wore a Rolex, and I wore hand-me-down Lands' End jeans from my cousin Ginny and fake Teva shoes from Walmart that I was secretly ashamed of. I pretended not to notice my dad's tall, orange, sixteen-ounce plastic cup filled with Johnnie Walker Red, ice, and water sloshing by his stick shift. He used a cup from my mom's alma mater: Randolph-Macon Woman's College. Though my parents were divorced, he stayed married to that cup for the next twenty years. It didn't fit in the car's cup holder, so it was perched on the smooth beige leather by the stick.

My eyes stayed on the cup. I knew it was his third drink that day, and my insides began to get hot. I am not sure if it was because I knew that with any fast turn, I may get showered with ice-cold whiskey, or because I could tell he was loose in a way that scares me even now. But I pretended I was not scared to be in the car with him. Year after year, it was the same routine. When he had three, he went far away. I knew not to disturb him then. With one, he was fun. With two, he loved you. With three, let him be. So I sat quietly, and I focused on holding my breath so as to not let the fear swallow me whole.

At age eight, I sat in the lobby at my ballet school, the Ruth Mitchell Dance Theatre, pretending not to be distraught. My mom was an hour and a half late to pick me up. She was a full-time working mom doing the best she could to solo parent and make sure I could do things like ballet. It just meant I had to wait for her as she drove the rush-hour drive from Atlanta to pick me up. Each minute that went by without her black Honda Accord appearing heated up my insides as if I were a tiny copper tea kettle on a stovetop nearing a boil. I held my breath, hoping I would become invisible and that the boiling would stop. The receptionist with the short silver hair looked at the clock, then at me. I could tell she was about to say something, so I pretended to read my social studies homework. But in the last hour and a half, I had already done all my homework. I was eight, after all, and didn't have that much to do.

Eventually, the woman said, "We close soon. Are you sure she's coming? Do you need to call another family member or a neighbor?"

Our neighbors were not people we spoke to much, except to wave at them from our driveway. And as far as family went, my uncle had rescued us enough times, and I knew better than to call him at dinner time. It was just me and Mama. So I smiled and laughed, pretending to be a fun, carefree child instead of the child with the boiling insides, and said, "Yes, she is coming. She's on a big important project at work and driving in from the city. She'll be here soon!"

I held my breath to keep the inside of me from boiling over into the room and looked down at the map of the colonial South in my textbook, pretending to study it even though it was now too dark in the room to see. The sun had set. My insides were crumbling. This had become my routine. It was what must happen so I could study dance and learn how to sit with the heat and hold my breath in just a way so I couldn't feel anything.

Around age ten, my dad warned me that fat women were not desirable, so I started pretending to not be hungry in front of him, ever. And if I slipped and allowed myself to feel hungry and really eat, he would notice and say, "Be careful. You will get fat," which meant, "Be careful. You will not be loved." And since I already didn't feel loved, the prospect of feeling even *more* unloved was scary enough for me to keep pretending I was not hungry until I was about twenty-eight years old.

I also betrayed my body and avoided feeling her truth by trying to be thin for a very long time. At my height, five feet, two and a half inches, being thin was required. Having a full body, ample thighs, and a belly like a full moon just wasn't allowed, said the unspoken rules in my Protestant, white, middle-class world. So, starting at age twelve and into high school, I avoided feeling fat with the occasional packet of brown laxatives, each smaller than an M&M, that left a sweet taste in my mouth before I swallowed. And I spent nights half asleep on the bathroom floor waiting for the cramps to begin and for my insides to spew out so I could feel relief and pain safely, alone. Then I spent days staying hungry without telling a soul.

At age thirteen, wearing navy blue cheerleading shorts rolled up to expose the soft underpart of my butt cheeks, with braces and freckles and frizzy hair that couldn't be tamed, I discovered that cigarettes helped me avoid feeling pain. Someone passed me a Camel Light, and my body started to tremble with a buzz I had never felt. I was able to breathe and relax for the first time, which spurred my bowels to make a move. Leaning against a giant oak in the woods with the rope swing dangling in the breeze, the sun set over me as I passed the cigarette back and forth with Lanie and Camila. They seemed more interested in talking about boys than smoking, but I was feeling in a way I never had before.

Tobacco kept the pain *and* love at bay because I didn't trust either of those things. It formed a barrier between me and all the feelings. When I smoked, I could detach. I could finally rest. Puffs of smoke kept me safe by making a bubble around me. I looked like a cool girl, but she was a cover-up for the truth: that I was a sad, lonely girl pretending to be cool. Underneath the cool surface, my insides were still boiling, and under that, I felt unloved and afraid.

These are just some of the ways I learned to stuff down my feelings from a young age, deepening a coping mechanism that would inevitably fail. How many of us have done this at some point in our lives? How many of us are still doing it? When we avoid our sincere feelings, we sacrifice our true selves. We leave a part of ourselves behind. We abandon our truth on behalf of others because we are ashamed, or we are afraid we will lose something if we reveal our deepest selves.

I was lucky, though, to have found my feelings again, my own heart, my true self, and my connection to life when I went to school for art, theater, and writing. It was my savior. That was where I learned to feel and breathe again. I didn't consciously know why I needed to go, but something inside of me knew: "There is a whole life available where we open to the moment, breathe, and dare to feel without numbing ourselves." This is loving. This is connecting. This is the openhearted spiritual path where we let go of control and enter into life.

At eighteen, I was at NYU, standing in front of the class in a second-floor acting studio on 21st and Broadway. It was an area of town where you could find Chinese-made wholesale goods pouring out of tiny shops, like strange wind-up toys that float in the tub, colored beanies, and knockoff aviator sunglasses. I stood in front of the class with my long, curly hair with blondish highlights and brown roots that betrayed me, attempting to breathe. Stephanie, my wiry, spritely teacher, studied the way I did so. Intentionally breathing in front of a room of students who all stared at me felt like torture. I tried to do it, though. After all, I was paying a lot of money to attend the school. I, not my parents. I.

She watched me breathe and said, "You are an inward breather. We cannot see or feel you breathing. You are breathing inside yourself. Your belly and chest never move. You must start breathing into your belly if you want to deeply feel."

I was stunned. How on earth could she possibly know that? See that? How had she discovered my coping strategy for life, then told the whole class? I held my breath even more in that moment, trying to appear calm and not completely exposed.

I told her it was because I was a ballerina from age four to fourteen, so I learned to hold my belly in. But I knew the truth. I had been practicing not breathing and becoming invisible and not feeling since I was little. I was very good at it. And she was now telling me that I must stop, which was terrifying.

Over time Stephanie and my other teachers taught me to breathe and, in turn, to feel. I was mortified at first, but I did it. With breathing came embarrassment, tears, and rage, and I poured them into my acting and writing. That way, no one could notice how much of the pain was mine. I quickly gave it a new home, acting as complex characters in Shakespeare and Brecht plays, madly shaking my body in experimental performance art, writing plays about what I cared about, and taking self-portraits as different goddesses and archetypes on 35 mm film.

One day at the acting studio, I stood in line for the bathroom behind a woman who had bothered me from day one. She had hairy armpits and wore torn sweatpants and sat on the floor instead of using a chair, plus she was loud and looked feral. Her freedom and confidence scared me. She rubbed her belly, then turned to me and said, "I am so constipated."

When she spoke those words, the air shattered around me. I had been constipated since I was five. When my parents split, my mom and I moved far from my father, safety and security shattered for me, my dad became mean and cold, and we became poor and needy. I learned to hold in my breath, rage, and grief. And now, in line for the bathroom, under fluorescent lights, this woman spoke my truth out loud.

I opened my mouth and heard the words, "Me too," come out.

A warmth flooded between us. A kinship. We were not alone! We were both women trying not to pretend, and yet our bowels betrayed us. Our bowels said, "I am full of things I cannot release. Things I have held in. Things I am afraid of. Ways I have pretended." We spoke of our favorite ways to unclog our bowels, from enemas to psyllium husks to Smooth Move tea, and there in that bathroom line we found a friend in one another. I had been a slave to perfection and thinness, holding it all together and in, and I could tell she had begun to escape this malady; she seemed a few steps ahead of me, so I felt I could breathe around her.

Nearly twenty years later she is still one of my dear friends.

Avoiding feeling was like a virus that would go latent at times, and I would think it was gone, feeling free for a few months or years when I wasn't avoiding my feelings. But then it would show up again out of nowhere—in my loving, in my sexing, in my relationship to my body, and right smack dab between me and God.

I found yoga and meditation when I was nineteen, and I discovered I could sidestep my pain with the practices that were trending in New York City in 2003. I found a deep calm and more breath when I moved my body at the Tuesday night yoga classes at the community center on Avenue C, while Paz, the Jewish teacher with dreads, adjusted my posture and taught me the nadi shuddhi breath. I felt that yoga asked me to breathe the pain away gently and be egoless and clean and holy, a bit like my childhood Christian values, but this time with incense and a bow that said, "The Divine in me honors the Divine in you."

I found refuge in spirituality. Behind those practices I neatly tucked my feelings, until one day someone saw me hiding there.

At twenty, I stood in front of a room of fellow students at school, and my teacher Deborah stared at me. She was tall and mighty, with wispy blonde hair, Swedish clogs, and many large rings on all her fingers. She oozed sex, power, and strength in a way that both terrified and inspired me. I had just performed something called a "private moment," in which I was instructed to pull down all my proverbial masks, to stop acting and feel big feelings and be deeply revealed in front of the class. She looked me in the eye. Something about her gaze told me I didn't do it right.

"Stop hiding behind your spirituality. I don't buy it," she said. "Who are you beneath all that?"

My lip began to tremble.

"Yes," she said. "That's it, stay with that."

In front of the room, I crumbled. I was exhausted from stuffing and holding down all the feelings. My exhaustion came as heaves and screams and my hands beating against the wooden floor of the studio. For five minutes I let them all see who I was when I was not holding in my feelings. And when my time was up, I walked quietly back to my seat, feeling scared, naked, exposed, humiliated, and nauseous. How dare anyone notice that I was avoiding my feelings in my spiritual life! No one was supposed to find me there. I stopped breathing so I could stop feeling for the rest of the school day and ran home as fast as I could after class so I could let it out in privacy.

Somehow, I knew what had happened in class was important. I'd been holding it all in for so long and there was now an opening, and I knew I must take it. I laid in my dark, lofted bed in my apartment on 13th Street and Avenue B where the mice scurried on the floor, too busy to see me crying in the dark. I breathed. I cried like I had never cried before. I was so angry at my teacher for unraveling me, exposing me. I was so angry at myself for incessantly holding in my true feelings, hiding my broken heart, my "I am not okay," and the scared little girl I abandoned all those years ago by stifling her breath. But besides being angry and heartbroken, I also felt something new. I started to feel space in my chest where there were once knots. I felt tingling where there was once numbness. I felt warmth in my belly that said, "Yes, that is it, my Love!" And I felt something I'd only felt a few times: free.

That was the beginning of something for me.

A glimmer of my own truth crystalizing in my body and coming out of hiding.

A start to a lifelong journey and a spiritual path that included all of me.

A nod to a calling to devote myself to the art of feeling, to express the pain and beauty in my heart as art no matter what, to not pretend as a defense, to love my body even though it is sometimes difficult, to breathe deep always, and to speak and write about it. All of it.

These days, I can catch myself holding in my truth because something will *feel* off. It is usually in the space of social niceties where I catch myself with a fake smile. Or I catch myself saying yes to too many things when I want to say no. Or I go along with what my partner wants because I want to please him. Because I want him to keep loving me. When this happens, I feel a twinge of something in my gut that says, "You are off your center. This is not your truth."

I've learned that this feeling is important and that I must listen to it. It's a clench in my belly where my breath goes shallow, and I lose sight of myself for a moment. When I feel this, it is like a part of me is waving and saying, "I need your help!" So, I take a simple pause, stop what I am doing, take a deep breath, feel, and get curious. I ask: *Where am I pretending? Where did I just abandon my truth?* When I can see it, which may take a few minutes, I feel into what is under the clench, even if it is uncomfortable. Am I scared I won't be loved if I am honest? Am I angry? Am I tired and ready to go home? Am I withholding a deep desire that I am ashamed of? I feel into the inquiry of what TRUTH is under my holding.

And then I hold my Scared Little Girl Self close and tell her I love her and that I've got her, and I remind her that we don't need to do that anymore.

When we avoid our true feelings, we sacrifice our true selves. We leave a part of ourselves behind. We abandon our truth on behalf of others because we are ashamed or afraid we will lose something if we reveal our deepest selves. But in this process, we forfeit discovering who we really are. We stay in the safe zone and don't widen and deepen as embodied souls. We stay small. When we commit, instead, to the messy and real revelation of our truth, we expand. We break down walls in our loving. We put down the ideas of who we thought we were. We feel powerful and close to our own blood and guts. Here, in the wide-open messy realness, we find our home, which was in us all along.

Dare *to* Feel

REFLECTIONS

Throughout the book I will provide questions for reflection. Contemplate these in your mind and heart silently, or answer them in a journal or wherever you keep your musings on the path. Reflecting on my story in this chapter of learning not to feel, consider:

- In what areas of life do you abandon the truth of what you are feeling and hold it all in because it feels like it is too much, too intense, or too disruptive?

- When have you chosen to leap into deep feeling, even when you were uncertain of what would happen if you did? How did it feel to open up in that way?

- Reflect on a time when you expressed your truth, even if it was messy or intense, and it was actually a gift to the people around you.

- Do you have a vision for where you could leap MORE into feeling instead of pretending you are okay when you are not?

- Have you ever used the mask of spirituality to bypass your humanity and the depth of feeling the moment was calling you into? For example, have you ever used an attitude of "good vibes only" to bypass something painful?

RITUAL FOR FEELING

You will also find rituals to anchor you in the teachings of the stories throughout the book. They are designed to help put the spiritual concepts I introduce into practice. A ritual can be any moment you imbue with intention, where you step outside of your casual self and attempt to enter into a numinous space of devotion, prayer, and mystery. When I am entering into a ritual space, I like to turn off my phone, clean my space, and begin with some deep breaths.

These rituals will be best practiced when you have some privacy and aren't in a rush. I love doing rituals early in the morning, in candlelight, before the sun rises. Some people love doing them before bed. It is completely up to you. Just carve out enough space so you can take your time, and work privately so you don't feel the need to explain what you are doing to anybody.

Here, your ritual is to write down ten reasons you tend not to face big feelings when they arise in you. Dig into this, even if it means getting really deep, raw, embarrassing, and honest with yourself.

(Examples: "If I feel my anger, I may break a window!" or "People will think I am crazy if they learn how insecure I am.")

This list represents your blocks to daring to feel. Have compassion for the voice inside that is trying to "keep you safe" by doing these things. Ask yourself: "Am I ready to begin to release these beliefs?"

Once you have your list, take some deep breaths, and prepare to let it all go. Then burn the page! I've been doing burning rituals for over twenty years, and they are a classic way to transform energy and say goodbye. You can do this over the stove, in a pot, or in a fireplace. As you let your list burn, feel the fires of transformation ignite change in your life. Feel free to incorporate burning rituals into your life on a regular basis. The night before a new moon is a good time for this. Use herbs in your fire, use song, and make the ritual your own. You can also just visualize a burning ritual in your mind's eye.

TO BE A WOMAN WHO DOESN'T PRETEND

To be a woman who doesn't pretend.
Who doesn't fake a smile.
Who never abandons her truth.

To be a woman
who stays in the boiling discomfort of a pregnant pause
before rushing in with a pleasantry.

To be a woman
who dares to sit quietly
like an ancient Egyptian cat
rather than become catty
or clucky.

To be a woman
who dares to feel pleasure
in public,
not as a performance,
but because hiding it
would be betrayal to the soul.

To live outside of the
"What are they thinking of me?"
and
"Do they like me?"

But to let yourself be unliked,
raw, and shining!

To be a glistening heart
that says no
when it must.

And that drops heavy tears onto tables,
and a lover's chest,
smears of mascara onto crisp linen . . .

Because not to cry
would be a lie.

And you are ready to live a life of no pretending.

When It Feels Safer to Be Alone

With my JanSport backpack strapped across my shoulders, I slipped in the dark through the neighbor's yard, the neighbor I had overheard Mama saying was a "flasher," who had apparently stood naked at his front door while Miss Kathy, the neighbor on the other side, walked her toy poodles one morning. Holding my breath, I walked the length of his fence through his poison ivy–spotted mess of a yard, into the Kennedy's perfectly manicured one, and straight up to their front door. It was 7:30 am, and my mom had to start her drive to Atlanta to be at the law firm where she worked as a paralegal by 9:00 am, so she asked Mrs. Kennedy if I could sit in their home and catch a ride with their family to school every morning.

I was six, and just six months prior I had moved with my mama away from my dad and our home in Miami to Marietta, Georgia, where my uncle and his family lived. Marietta was nothing like Miami. It was covered in Civil War monuments, Protestant churches, and strip malls, and the ocean was nowhere in sight. I was in the middle of what I would later call the biggest heartbreak of my life. Now, at age thirty-eight, with gray hairs peeping through my auburn curls, I can say that after suffering a great many heartbreaks, the one where I lost my father, and my mother in a way, too, was the worst. My mom went from being available to make me PB&Js and take afternoon walks with me to working sixty to seventy hours a week. My dad was so angry at my mother for "stealing me" from him that he took his anger out on me for the next twenty-five years, until I was thirty-two years old and decided to forgive him because, well, he was just broken-hearted, too. And so, in their divorce when I was five, I lost them both.

But back to the Kennedy's house. My breath was still shallow after traipsing through Flasher's yard in the dark Georgia morning, where the sun was just peepin' (pun intended) from behind the ridge of pine trees. Dew gathered on the burgundy Dodge minivan that was cuddled beside a black Lexus sedan in the driveway. I hesitated before ringing the doorbell. The shame I felt was heavy, like a lead suit that covered my six-year-old frame. If you listened real close, you could hear my bones break from that weight. I rang the doorbell, even though they always told me to "Just come in." Mrs. Kennedy answered and invited me in. She looked perfect: leggy, with a dirty blonde bob and a removed sort of tenderness toward me, like she felt sorry for me but was too busy with her family to stop and sit with that pity. One of her eyes had a distorted pupil, like an art piece, with a black blob that colored outside the line of her pupil and into the white. Apparently, her sister accidentally stabbed her in the eye while they were "horsing around" as kids.

The Kennedys were amidst their morning routines as usual. Mr. Kennedy was handsome: his hair was perfectly combed to the side, he sported a wide, white-toothed grin, and he wore a suit and tie that said, "Off to the office!" They had three perfect children who sat drinking orange juice and eating waffles: two boys—Jason, who was five, and Matt who was three—who were blond and always smiling; and one girl, Ashley, who was eight and soft and gentle, with perfectly square white teeth. I sat on the couch waiting for them, feeling my skin crawl with invisible fire ants. Something about experiencing that much normalcy and family and love was terrifying. Also, I felt like an imposition, a voyeur into their mornings. Perhaps mornings were sacred to them, and there I was, contracted into a macaroni shape with my head dipped, making a dent on their couch as I wore pilled cotton hand-me-downs from my cousin and *Power Rangers* played on the TV. I kept my gaze averted downward or pretended to watch. I hated kids' TV, and I hated being in that room. I missed the Miami sun and my dad's boat, the Spanish speaking, our big house with my Juliet balcony, how I could run free down the street to Arielle's house and swim in her big pool and eat fruit snacks while the AC blasted in her bedroom and we watched *The Goonies*, which we were probably too young for.

Every morning Mrs. Kennedy asked me if I wanted some juice or a waffle, and every morning I politely declined. I typically ate Raisin Bran with skim milk alone in the kitchen while Mama curled her hair and put on her law firm outfit. I was too proud to accept their Eggo Waffles and fresh OJ, too ashamed. I was a kid whose heart was broken. I was far from home. I was amidst strangers while my mother worked all day and into the nights and my father lived hundreds of miles away. But even though their love felt far away and inconsistent like snow in the South, I loved them dearly. I yearned for them mightily. I hoped and prayed and wished for them. I missed my dad's Johnny Walker Red breath and bellowing laughter. The way he perched one arm over his belly when he danced the Lambada. The way he talked loud in the grocery store and said hello to everyone like he was the mayor of Coral Gables, Miami. I missed Mom's blood-red nails and svelte body from her BodyWorks workouts, her sky-blue Mustang, and her Andreas Vollenweider cassette tapes I called the "twinkle twinkle" music. The way she used to put bows in my hair.

But now in Georgia things were different. I imagined Mama, age thirty-three, in her 1990 Honda Accord spending an hour and some change in traffic to Atlanta after getting her six-year-old dressed for school and off to the neighbor's house. All day she would file away paperwork for one of the partners at the firm and get home to me by 6:30 or so. Did she think of me? Was her heart also breaking from the divorce and leaving her baby with strangers all the time? Later she would fetch me at the afterschool daycare for underprivileged kids at the church, where I was the only white girl. Eventually, when I got a little older, she would find me home alone every day after school.

Alone.

All those years of aloneness formed a hard shell around my heart. I never wanted to be left again, so when it came to love, I learned to do

the leaving first. That's why it hurt so much when I tried to love someone and they either didn't return it or didn't stay. They didn't know it,
but it had taken me the courage of a rosebud, pushing through tight
green coverings after a frostbitten, snow-covered winter, to give them
my open heart. I was actively going against the gripping fear in my
body with every moment of loving or choosing trust. And when they
were too stuck in their own pain to notice my gesture or they ignored
it altogether, my heart snapped back like a door left open during a
windstorm. There was a loud bang, and usually everyone felt it. It was
easier to stay closed, controlled, and managed than to let in the wild
unknown of someone else's love. Isn't that why so many people stay
alone? They say, "Oh, I just haven't met the one." But don't we know
that we who haven't surrendered to love are scared? We feel we may die
if we let someone in that deep because we didn't get the right imprint
as kids that it's a safe thing to do. Somewhere deep within, we think,
"If love always feels like it's going to leave, then why invite it in?" So,
we stay "safe" by not letting ourselves surrender control to love.

But this "safety" isn't truly living. It's living behind walls and not
letting the heart be seen or touched deeply by the pain and joy of intimacy. If intimacy is what hurts that precious heart, then being alone
can feel much safer! It makes perfect sense. But one day, if we allow
it, we see that all we want is the bliss of loving, the pain of the deep
surrender to love, and the eventual loss and devastation that comes at
some point along the journey of loving. Even *that* we decide is worth
it. When we say yes to love, even though we know we cannot control
the outcome, it is a brave, brave act. This makes us powerful! Even in
our extreme vulnerability. We are stepping up to life even though we
know we may get hurt. Like a dancer who dances after a knee injury.
Or someone who has the courage to drive a car after an accident. You
could avoid cars your whole life or take some deep breaths and go on
that road trip: say your prayers, buckle your seatbelt, and surrender.

)cess of centering a new internal voice is one of the scar-
iost vulnerable things, an identity shift, a transfiguration.
the back seat a part of you that's been creating a safe bubble

for you, the part of you that has been the reason for your so-called success. Offering her as a sacrifice to Love. Integrating her wisdom. Because you know she has done her job well, and she is in you, and she built a lot for you, but she doesn't need to be the leader anymore.

And what a scary thing to do to try and dethrone that part of you!

Crossing the threshold into newness is very risky. You may fail. And that's part of it. That's part of the process. To not stay stuck, to move, to attempt the journey and trust wherever you land.

Dare *to* Feel

REFLECTIONS

- Where and how do you block love from finding you? Where do you close off to potential love from life, strangers, the world, out of fear? This could be as simple as saying no to compliments instead of receiving them as love. This could be an inability to take in an offer from someone to help you out. Think deeply.

- Where and when has your heart been broken so deeply that the imprint has prevented you from risking being hurt again? Has this happened multiple times? What were the major ones? How do these heartbreaks impact you daily?

- What is aloneness to you? What is loneliness to you? Does one or the other feel more comfortable? More like a habit you fall into?

- Did any events from your past create a reality for your present that you are ready to graduate from? A way of receiving love that feels like it needs an upgrade?

RITUAL FOR THE LITTLE ONE WITHIN

Write a letter to the Little One within you from the perspective of your Adult Self. Say what you wish you could say to the child within you. Shower them with love, apologies, wishes, whatever comes up for you. Imagine you could have a direct line to them. If you have a picture of yourself as a kid that you connect to, use this as a visual aid to help you feel the vulnerability of your younger self.

Then spend a few minutes in the mirror consciously connecting to your Adult Self. Put on a song. Dim the lights. Gaze into your own eyes. What have you learned that you'd like to pass on to your inner Little One? What do you notice about who you are now? Add that to the letter. Perhaps you want to let them know that they are safe, that you've got their back, and that it's okay to play. Take your time with your letter and keep it somewhere you can refer to it any time it feels safer to shut down and isolate. Next time your Little One decides to say no to something "scary," locate the Adult Self who you saw in the mirror and who can hold them and guide them as they dare to feel.

STAY CLOSE

Stay close to your heart,
even if it hurts.

Stay raw and real,
even when it seems uncouth.

Stay deep and true,
even if it makes you messy and strange.

Stop playing it safe,
even if it is scarier
to walk toward edges and cliffs.

Make friends there!
Catch ideas there!
Be free there!
Live full . . .
if you dare!

Because this is your chance.
Today!
Now!
Not tomorrow!
But here,
now
!

Blood.
Guts.
Glory.

Love
flag
waving
in
the
wind.

When Emotion Has
Nowhere to Go

When I was thirteen, I went to Brazil for the summer with my dad and his girlfriend at the time, Ione (pronounced ee-O-neigh). She was Brazilian, like my father, also thin and blonde, spry, and she carried a kayak on her back, drank Bud, and spoke crassly. I appreciated her traveling with us because I could disappear a little more that way. She was a buffer between my father and my prepubescent awkwardness. I wished I was back home in Marietta, Georgia, sitting beside the pool in the Hardage Farms subdivision, flirting with boys, eating popsicles that turned my tongue blood red, rolling my shorts up to reveal browning yet freckled young thighs, and sitting in air-conditioned movie theaters chewing on gummy bears with my friends while the fireflies and cicadas danced and sang outside. Instead, I was someplace foreign. Before cell phones and internet, I had just myself, a few books, and a full summer ahead in Brazil with my father. I know it sounds exotic, but for a preteen, it was disorienting to skip into another culture. That was, until I found Malibu rum and started going to the teen clubs and making out with boys. Then summers in Brazil got a lot more fun as I forgot how far away from home I was and how lonely I felt, and lost myself in crushes and nights out dancing.

My family in Brazil took naps after lunch as a daily rite. My grandma would lay down twice a day, once at 11 am and again around 3. My dad held this custom and still does to this day. On the first day we landed in Brazil with Ione, she sauntered into the living room with her long, spiderlike legs that emerged from running shorts that screamed 1997 and said, "We are going to take a nap." I was seated on the upholstered, burgundy, flower-printed couch reading a book, with a view of the city to my right from our seventh-floor window.

Seconds after Ione announced that she and my father were taking a nap, her moans began. Since my parents divorced when I was five, I didn't remember ever hearing those type of animal sounds from my mother. They were foreign to me, like the sounds of a dying cow trapped in barbed wire, similar to what I had seen on a farm in Brazil with my father and his friends. I always quietly wondered how the cow had gotten there. Was it trying to escape? Had it lost its mind for a moment? Or did it simply wonder what those little spikes felt like?

Hearing Ione make the sounds of a dying cow caused my body to feel a mix of shock, confusion, and fear. Of course, I had seen sex scenes in movies, so I knew on some level that they were having sex. But I had never heard the sounds in real life. Something in my body clenched and froze like a deer in headlights. Something in me wanted to flee, but I had nowhere to go; the apartment was small.

Then something instinctual took over. I walked into the kitchen, with its white tiled floors and overhead fluorescent lighting, a place where no one had ever cooked. It was void of heart. Hearth. Warmth. It was clinical. Sterile. Empty. I opened a cabinet and saw everything my dad had purchased to make the apartment a home, though they had never been used. There were rows of brand-new cabinets with stacks of plates and glasses that no lips had ever touched. Silverware that had never attended a dinner party or heard the sounds of effulgent laughter. So, when I procured a tall clear glass in my thirteen-year-old hands, fingers wrapped around the cool sides, I felt like I was giving that glass a purpose. I felt as though it was entering into a ritual of sacrifice with me as time slowed. I had nowhere to put my screams, my anger, the bubbling rage within me, the confusion, the displacement, the "I wanna go home," the "Can the adults in my life, for once, treat me like a kid?" so I placed all those screams from my child heart into the glass through my hands wrapped around the cool, hard surface. And though I was never good at sports, though no one had officially taught me how to throw, my arm was ready to do its best bidding.

With the fluorescent lights illuminating the scene like a small stage suspended in time, I pulled my arm back and raised the tall glass to the sky, ready to make my offering to the gods with my heart's pain crying for help and an exorcism with each loud moan I heard. I threw the glass onto the white tiles and stood still as it shattered around me into a thousand tiny pieces. I took a deep breath, and something within me opened. There was release where everything had been tied into knots. Where things hadn't made sense, there was now a little bit of clarity.

I stood there, and I waited. I just knew this was the part where the sound would shatter their lovemaking, where they would remember there was another human there. *She is tiny still. She needs adults still. We got carried away with ourselves.* I just knew this was the part where someone would remember I was a child who needed her parents. This was the part where things would change. I stood still amidst my conjuring spell, waiting, holding the pose. Minutes went by, and even more minutes went by. And they kept going. The sounds of the dying cow escalated into the sounds of a woman birthing a child, which I had seen on TV. The huffs and puffs and grunts and moans. Hyperventilating. The anger rose within me again. It was instinctual and beyond my control. My body churned fire and ice. I looked into the cabinets, and I asked for another volunteer with a penetrating gaze. I pulled another tall glass down into the grip of a pain-filled human's hand, and I pulled my arm back like the pitcher at the Atlanta Braves games I went to as a kid. An invisible crowd cheered me on as I wrenched my arm back, took a deep breath, and pitched the glass onto the milk-white tiles.

Little shards of glass scattered everywhere. Little shards of my heart shattered everywhere. And I waited. The moans were high-pitched now. I waited. They must have heard the glass shatter. How could they not? They were coming, any minute now. I waited still, standing in the middle of my shattered heart. They were coming. I just had to wait.

I waited under the fluorescent lights for what felt like hours, and no one arrived. I decided that yet again I must be invisible, so I found the broom in the closet, never once used, and I swept up the pieces of my heart, little shards of me scattered about. Slowly I swept, and slowly I wept. I swept and swept until all the little pieces of me were in the dustpan, then I put them into the trash can and sat back on the couch with my book. There was more space inside of me now. I had moved something out of me and into a ritual that no one had taught me, and it felt like something. It wasn't a happy end, but it was movement, an exorcism of sorts, a response that got to live through the body and soul.

Life is fucking messy. Humans are messy. And we can choose to let those moments of chaos and mess tear us down, or instead to face them boldly, doing what we can, walking the path, staying the course. We don't hide from the truth of our pain, our rage, our fear. Even if we can take just one little step toward honesty and standing up for what we need or what we know to be true.

These moments when we stand instead of collapse are soul making. We get to see what we are made of. The parts of us that must stand up, must speak up, must move the energy and pain, pouring it into poetry or art or dance, or breaking glass, or singing, or sports, or cooking, or screaming. Emotions need a channel. When they just sit within us, they build walls around our hearts and minds that calcify and make us sick, turning to stone in our bellies and making headaches that don't go away. **When we feel the moment, as tough as it is, we stay free.**

Dare *to* Feel

REFLECTIONS

- Is there a feeling trapped in your body from a moment you felt someone hurt you? Could you give that feeling a gesture, a movement, an action?

- Imagine your parents as kids and teenagers. Did they have access to the tools for self-awareness that you do now? Can you accept them as imperfect humans (like you!) who were trying to do their best with the tools they had available? What would that look like?

- Has anything happened to you that has given you an "identity" that you are ready to release? Perhaps being the caregiver of everyone in the family, or the overachiever, or the martyr, or invisible one, for example. Is it possible to see whatever happened to you from a different perspective? If not, that is okay. If you can start to see yourself outside of that old identity, notice what that feels like, and consider who you are without that old you.

RITUAL FOR POWER

Set your ritual space. Light a candle. Put on some soft tunes or sit in silence. Sit upright on a cushion with your spine straight. Take a few deep breaths to ground and slow down. Visualize a scenario where you were not able to leave the room, to stand up for yourself, or where you were denied agency in any other way. Be discerning. There is no need to go right to your most intense experience of this; start with something small and see what feels safe in your body. Begin to dare to feel the emotions of feeling oppressed or disrespected. Feel the heat or sadness in your body and breathe into it. Breathing is truly key to feeling fully, and staying grounded while you do so.

Then, visualize yourself speaking up for what you need. Feel your power and agency. Now allow your body to leave that space in your imagination; see yourself running, moving, leaving the scene, and physically saying "no." Not escaping or fleeing but choosing to leave after having spoken up. If emotions arise, that is okay. Let the tears come. If anger feels present, feel free to growl or moan. If the emotions still feel heavy when your visualization is complete, put on some music and shake your body and make some sounds. Then sit and ground with some deep breaths. Drink some water and take care of you.

HEART WARRIOR

To be a
Heart Warrior
in this world
can be
terrifying!

While some say,
"Be calm,
be peaceful,
stay chill,
stay namaste!"

A Heart Warrior
says, "I am ready to enter the fire!"
baring the soul
and risking it all.

A Heart Warrior
discerns
between reactive
waves of emotions
and emotions as
portals to liberation
and purification.

And then
screams,
protects,
speaks up,
shouts,
cries,
moans,
groans,
even
as the rug of comfort
gets ripped out
from under them!

And then the Heart Warrior
lays there gutted and broken
and still
opens their heart!

Still loves,
still gives,
still laughs,
open,
gutted,
bloody,
free.

Most people will not dare enter this path
of soul nudity
and exposure.

They will not let their bleeding heart be seen.

But the brave ones will
surrender to
baring all,
heart
and
soul!

And they will even beg for more, crying:

"Beloved!
crack me open,
push out all my forgetting
until I laugh and laugh
as liberated love.
Purify me
and open this heart!
I am yours!"

Each wave of riveting passion,
each tear,
each smile,
gutted,
open,
free.

When Fear Gets Stuck

It was spring in New York City. Didn't Frank Sinatra sing about springtime in New York? Someone did. Someone noticed the cherry blossoms and magnolias and the spark in the eyes of every human on the street who could finally shed the heavy layers of a cold winter, bare their shoulders as if they were showing off Cartier rings, and sit in cafés as if street-side sipping and dining were the hottest new inventions. Sex and flirting are reborn and reinvigorated every spring in New York City, and celebrating street side and in parks is given its full debut.

I was nineteen, and I had left my childhood home of Marietta, Georgia, a year prior. I felt like I was on top of the world. New York provided me with constant adventure, romance, art, and theater. I got student-priced tickets to *Medea* starring Fiona Shaw, and I saw Edward Norton in a play on Union Square. I ran into Liv Tyler on the street, and I discovered Matthew Barney at the Guggenheim. My heart was pumped up like a helium balloon, and my spirit was like a neon sign, buzzing and bright twenty-four hours a day. No matter that I was in college on student loans, making eight dollars an hour working two part-time jobs through NYU's work-study program as a babysitter for Upper West Side families with fathers who hit on me. My clothes were from Goodwill, but luckily that was mega cool at the time. My Chuck Taylors were dirty, and my nails were chipped. My yellow sports Discman rotated between Radiohead's *The Bends* and Bjork's *Greatest Hits*. I was freedom incarnate. It didn't matter that

I lived in a small room with two other girls, one of whom hadn't yet found a deodorant that still worked after her two-hour runs on the West Side Highway. No matter that we shared a small bathroom, and I bunked on top of one of them. I was living within a dream. I had never felt so alive in my life. Nothing mattered but the fact that my soul now had wings.

It was a chilly spring night that required a light jacket. I rode down the elevator from my dorm on the eighth floor, excited. I was off to see John Travolta speak to a small group of artists at the Stella Adler Studio of Acting. This was the place where I had finally learned to feel. This was the place where my teachers resurrected my breath and tears, where my walls were broken down, where I was able to let go of being self-conscious, where I found freedom in my body, where I broke free.

The Stella Adler Studio was a special place for me—a temple, a rehab center, a lab of soul—tucked away between 6th Avenue and Broadway on an unassuming street on the third floor. My amazing friends Matt and Dan were in the film department, and they tagged along to see John Travolta with me. We all piled into the studio elevator, and right before the doors could close, a very drunk girl named Bethany and three of her friends piled in. I counted fourteen of us altogether. I was sandwiched in the back between Matt and Dan. They were soft, they were young, and they loved me very much, perhaps in a way I had never been loved before. How could we love that much when we had only known each other for such a brief time in school? Somehow, we did. It was a strong love, a young love, a love that had me kissing each of them in those months without attachment or pressure, but simply from the desire of one creature to connect with another. My heart was one that had buried its scars. It was now naïve and open, a baby fawn heart hungry and willing, yearning and free.

When a heart has been broken and has closed, love softly and gently finds its way to it again and soothes it like a honey balm, like tears that have turned into blessings and made the scars go away for a while, a magical enchantment of forgetting the past and living in the now. This is healing that just comes. The healing you don't have to work so hard for. The healing that wraps itself around you with gentle arms that say, "You are safe now." Some healings have been forged in fire and require you to trudge through dark forests. But this heart healing came with the gentleness of spring blossoms, hands tucked inside each other, sloppy kisses, and mixtapes.

The elevator started its journey up to the third floor with all fourteen of us in it, then suddenly, between the second and third floor, it began to fall. Then it shook with a frightening plunk that clearly meant we were stuck. Of course, that's when we noticed the sign on the inside of the elevator that specified a weight limit we were clearly beyond. I could smell the red wine on Bethany's breath as she spoke loudly in the metal box we were trapped in. The combination of her wine breath and drunk slurs and the realization of being trapped made me want to eject even more quickly. We pushed the button to signal emergency services and waited. Matt and Dan each grabbed my hands as my body pressed against theirs. Between their hearts, my fear was held, quieted, calmed. The rest of the madness slipped away. Love invaded the anxiety, and our close bodies reminded me that I was okay.

I'm not sure if we were in that elevator for mere minutes or an hour, but the fire department eventually came. They opened the door and helped us climb out. I don't know how I did that climb, as it had always been an irrational fear of mine. I think I had seen this in a horror movie: someone was trying to get out of a stuck elevator and it suddenly dropped, splitting them in half. But as I looked up to climb out, John Travolta's beaming face greeted me. Two firefighters extended their hands to me, pulled me up and out, and John Travolta stood right in front of me. What happened next has stayed with me ever since, though in the haze of shock and after the years gone by my mind may have made up the best dialogue I can recall.

Tom, the head of my studio, asked, "Are you okay? Your face is white."

I nodded.

John Travolta looked at me and asked, "Where were you when it happened?"

I replied, "In the elevator."

"And where are you now?" he asked.

"Here."

"So where were you when it happened? And where are you now?"

He repeated those questions for a minute or so. At the time I could feel he was attempting to do something to me, but I didn't know what. Now, in retrospect, I think he was trying to help the trauma not stick to me. Trying to help me get back into my body and into the present moment, and out of the jam-packed elevator where I had likely dissociated in a panic. I wish his two minutes of work with me had worked; I probably needed an hour with him to have things not get stuck, but even then, I got the gist of how trauma sticks.

After a frightening event, many of us need a hug, a cup of tea, a shoulder to cry on, a space to say, "That was scary!" We need a space to be angry or sad and a space to deeply feel so nothing gets stuck. That night I just "kept calm and carried on" and wasn't able to tend to my own needs because I didn't know how to at the time. The imprint of my elevator fear got caught in my brain and body and hasn't ever officially left. Despite all the hypnotherapy, the exposure therapy, and time, I just don't like elevators. But what this means is I have to reach out my hand to someone I love when we are in the elevator. I have to let myself become not strong. I have to ask for community to support me. And if I'm solo, I just may have to take the stairs and be okay with that.

An animal instinctually shakes out trauma, but we humans tend to do the opposite. We often tense around it. We smush it down. We keep our attention on the tasks at hand, overriding the needs of our inner worlds and denying ourselves the time and energy it takes to stop and feel. We don't stop to tend to the "soft animal of our body," as poet Mary Oliver puts it, and so it becomes hard and those feelings get stuck. This is the new ask: that when hard things happen, we slow down and we feel. We hold ourselves or ask for help. We don't try and muscle through. We allow ourselves to have deep needs and to be seen in our vulnerability, knowing that this is essential to the healing process. That this is how we stay open to life and do not learn to close off out of fear.

Dare to Feel

REFLECTIONS

- What events in your life have imprinted deep fears within you? How many moments like this can you track? Contemplate how you might live differently if you dared to feel after a scary event.

- Choose one of these moments and craft what would have been the ideal response. For example: chamomile tea, three of your besties surrounding you, a hot Epsom salt bath, two days off work to recover. Next time something tough happens, try to implement this new plan.

- Has there been a John Travolta character in your life whom you wish you could thank for helping you dare to feel in a tough moment? What would you say to them now if you had the chance?

RITUAL FOR FACING FEAR

Have a friend accompany you in confronting something that makes your heart race. Maybe it's posting a vulnerable share on social media. Perhaps it's riding in an airplane or an elevator. Maybe it's saying hello to a hot stranger. Ask this friend to hold your hand (literally or metaphorically) as you dare to feel your fear of doing this difficult thing and have them remind you to breathe and stay in your body throughout. Take it slow. Cry if you need to. And after it's done, celebrate the fact that you dared to feel together!

THOSE WHO DARE TO HEAL

How do you have the courage
to allow yourself to fall apart under my watch,
to let yourself crumble under my gaze?

The way you drop your masks without pause brings me to my knees.

The way you unleash the storms of centuries with your cries
makes my lips tremble.

The way you so willingly share your heart
that has been trampled on,
stolen,
crushed,
and broken
so many times floors me.

The way you dare to re-enter your body,
the space you have deemed unsafe,
protected with barbed wire and yellow caution tape,
under investigation,
closed until further notice.

The way you say, "Fuck it."

My darling, it shakes me to my core.

Joy Warms a Timid Heart

After heartbreak or deep ruptures of trust, moments of joy can feel like rare gifts. To feel the goodness of joy we have to feel safe enough to be taken on a ride and trust it is going to feel good. Joy requires trust. Joy requires safety. Joy reaches into the sky and asks us to fly a bit, and sometimes we become so heavy and weighted that we say no again and again to the blissful expanse of joy. A broken heart may be reticent to feel joy, it may have developed scars that keep it "cool" and detached. Joy is not cool! It is childlike and free. It is wind in your hair, pee in your pants, making funny faces, snorts and cackles. It asks you to soar above the grief and heaviness, to expand your being, and to trust you will land safely after the journey. Joy asks you to surrender into its arms and let go of how you look and trust its waves. Joy feels like illuminations of light shot through the body, like voltage from the divine. Joy can cause such a high because it exists in an almost unlivable land, a place where, if you dared to linger too long, you could get burnt to a crisp from the sun of that high sensation. Perhaps you would become a shooting star. Perhaps you would miss out on the wildlife at the bottom of the ocean floor, the deep moments, rooted and slow. Joy is fast like lightning, a gift, a high, an epiphany.

In 2017, I visited one of my dear friends, Rebecca, who had just moved to Berkeley. She and her partner, Daniel, met at Burning Man and fell in love, and she moved from Seattle to San Francisco to be with him and go to school to be a therapist after a successful run at being a birth doula. I took a six-hour bus ride from downtown

LA to Berkeley, stared out the window aimlessly at farmlands, and landed in a co-op of sixty people who ate together, did activities together, and were all finishing grad school at UC Berkeley. Daniel was one of these people. Another dear friend, Shannon, had come from Seattle for the weekend as well, and we both slept on air mattresses in Rebecca and Daniel's room before we drove north to the hot springs for a girls' weekend.

I met Rebecca in college, and she introduced me to Shannon, who was an activist who had devoted herself to many causes and taught me endlessly about my white privilege, among other things. Back in 2006, this conversation hadn't yet invaded the mainstream, but Shannon was devoted to it. I loved her for that, and I am still grateful for it today. Rebecca introduced me to some things that changed my life: Brian Eno (whose ambient music I still listen to today), maté in the mornings (which is something my Brazilian grandpa drank but was new to me at age nineteen), tofu, and the magic of sitting on the floor instead of in chairs. Rebecca was fiery and strong when I met her, and she still is today, only now she boasts a softened mama's heart and a deep therapist gaze, which leads me back to my story.

Rebecca and Daniel took Shannon and me into an upstairs guest room that no one lived in, with bunk beds that felt like a college dorm room. The feeling in the air was homey.

"Close your eyes," Rebecca and Daniel said.

Shannon and I exchanged glances. What was going on? You never knew with Rebecca. She could come in with a cake and candles and say, "Because we weren't together on your birthday, let's have a party!" Or they could be putting on costumes and announcing we are going to a costume party. Regardless, we closed our eyes, and bubbles started to rise in my stomach. A pure excitement formed within me. It wasn't a nervous feeling, but it was active. My heart beat in a way I could clearly feel. Something was coming. My body's intuition knew it.

Rebecca and Daniel asked us to open our eyes. They were holding two big, blank pieces of cardboard. Were they doing some art for us? I wouldn't have put it past Rebecca to put on a theater show or performance art for us; in fact, that would have been very Rebecca. I took a breath.

They looked at each other with pure glee, and Rebecca said, "One, two, three . . ." They flipped the pieces of cardboard, which said, "We are having a baby!"

I started screaming uncontrollably, as if I was a teenage cheerleader with no self-awareness. My shrieks of pure joy were unbridled; they just came like a rainstorm, fast and determined. My small self disappeared as I expanded past the confines of my body and into the sky above.

Then came the tears, which dropped out of my eyes in droves. There were no other thoughts in that moment except my pure joy for them. That wave of joy lasted probably thirty seconds, and it lit me up from the inside. I remember it as if it were yesterday. Their baby boy is growing quickly, and the joy I feel to be his auntie is beyond words.

Rebecca often remarks on how touched she was at my pure expression of joy, how it meant so much to her. But the funny thing was, I couldn't control it, I didn't plan it, and I didn't fake it. I like to think of that as a moment of pure, spontaneous joy. But joy can come in a great many ways. When the heart has been hurt, it can feel timid about joy. The heart needs to be warmed by the presence of joy for a bit before it fully surrenders to it. Hurt can create a skeptical heart that doesn't trust the wild and big energy of joy. Looking at the picture in extremes, imagine a closed heart like a curmudgeon with a frown, saying "Bah humbug!" Imagine that closed heart being placed into a room of joyful children running free and chasing bubbles. It would be hard for that pained and hardened heart to stay closed. It would actually take more work to stay closed. The energy of joy is way bigger than whatever that curmudgeon experienced to become so closed. **Life is often trying to coax us out of our closure and pain. Often, before we get to the joy, there is a layer of grief that needs to be felt. Tears that need to be shed. But sometimes the joy comes in and sweeps through our pain, and it is a massive healer.**

Joy has found me laughing about nonsense with someone I love, choosing to be silly and do something unconventional, like dancing in a hotel lobby while everyone else is sitting and being civilized, like screaming at the top of my lungs with my besties to my favorite music on a road trip, or playing with a dozen puppies who lick my face with glee. Once, late at night, I was in Paris with a new potential love. We were sober and it was 2 am and I said, "I need to sleep." He replied, "Laughter will wake you." And he stripped naked and proceeded to run down the hallway of the hotel while I laughed uncontrollably. Then he challenged me to do the same. And I did it! I laughed like a little girl, though I was thirty-five, and we rolled on the ground laughing afterward. It may sound silly or trite, but in the moment, it was pure, free bliss and joy! It lifted my spirit into the realms of pure delight and tickled my heart alive.

Some cultures have ecstatic rituals and grief rituals that normalize and celebrate these states and create ceremony around them. People collectively soar to heights and drop into depths with traditions and songs and dances that support their journey. But for many of us, we didn't get a ritual or map to journeying into great heights and depths, and doing so without a guide or map can feel scary. And yet, if we don't journey there, we miss being a part of the great human circle of being and living. **And so, for the traditionless, for those of us who don't have the spiritual rituals in our own culture but are creating our own, we must dare to enter and embrace the states that life's experiences offer us.** The Goddess serves us a platter of opportunity, and though we don't know what we are getting, I suggest we say an enthusiastic "yes" to all of it: the drugs of human experience, free and plenty; the rituals we must create to hold these experiences; the new traditions; and the willing hearts we are cultivating, moment by moment.

When joy subsides, it leaves a mark on our hearts. Perhaps less pain is there now, perhaps the scar tissue has softened. The heart is freer.

Dare
to
Feel

REFLECTIONS

- Where do you resist joy, and why? In what times in your life has joy felt unreachable?

- What are your favorite pathways to experiencing joy? If nothing comes to mind, how do you think could experience more joy in your life?

- What rituals do you have around ecstatic states? Music you reach for? People you like to be around? Movies or shows you love? Memories you can reference? Consider these and write about them. Why do they feel so joyful to you? How does that joy and ecstasy live in your body?

- What culture do you create in your home around joy? Does your home feel supportive of a flow of joy? Is there music playing often that supports that? Do you and those you live with dance in the kitchen? Do you sing in the shower? Where and how do you feel safe to express joy in the home? Where is there room for more?

RITUAL FOR JOY

Create a prescription for joy for days when it feels far from reach and you need a reminder of the beauty and ecstasy of being alive. Using your responses to the reflection prompts above, write out the things that bring you back into your joy. Scan your past experiences for times when you have felt joy blooming in your body. Build out a list that you can keep handy. Perhaps it even goes on the fridge. Keep adding to this list over time, and let it become something you refer to when you want to access more joy in your life. Begin by adding some of those joy ingredients into your days for at least a month until they naturally integrate into your life.

LOOSEN THE GRIP

And then the times come when you just throw away the plans,
you take leaps that may seem "crazy" to others,
but you trust yourself and go for it.

You change the plane ticket to extend your trip,
you throw your schedule away,
you don't go to the workshop you had a ticket to.

Instead, you let life beckon you in;
you let the Flow carry you!

You let yourself not know what's next.

You surrender the Google calendar!
You get behind on the emails!
You risk looking silly!

You let yourself live BIG for a moment!

And the next thing you know, you're dancing
where no one else is
because you've worn gold boots for five days solid!

You're running naked down a hotel hallway at 3 am
stone cold sober,
as if you were eight years old.

And now you're feeling freer than you have in a LONG *time!*

And it feels like someone stuck their hand in your mind,
your heart,
and just started rearranging things!

Saying:
"Okay, let's stretch you open here.
Let's move this out a little wider.
Let's try a new way of thinking and being.
Let's get rid of this . . ."

And now, you're dropping the last layers of self-consciousness, of cool.
The little residue of "gotta look good" that keeps you small . . .

And now the Divine is flowing back
into all the places you held back
by being so "in control."
The grip is loosened.

Grace Heals a Heart

The elevator creaked on the way up to her second-floor apartment. "Why do we need to take the elevator when we're just going one floor up?" I would ask, but my dad liked to take the elevator—except when we wanted to surprise her. In those cases, we'd walk up the back steps and enter through the back door of the apartment and into the kitchen, where black beans cooked on the stove in dented aluminum pots and sheets hung on a clothesline. My dad would press his finger to his lips in a "Shhh!" gesture to alert Romilda, the housekeeper, that we were surprising my grandma. Then my robust, alpha, wild Brazilian dad would enter the living room where my grandma Lourdes, "vovó" in Portuguese, quietly watched a telenovela and crocheted at a high speed, a giant crucifix hanging on the wall behind her. He would spring up behind her, pouncing like a wild cat and startling her mightily.

"João Paulo!" she would exclaim. She'd be blazing mad, yelling, "Holy Mother of God!" and "Jesus Christ on a cross!" at him, and he'd howl with laughter. I'd stand there, hands folded tightly against my twelve-year-old body. I was often embarrassed by his loudness. My gentle Piscean temperament stood in direct contrast to his robust, earthy Taurus energy. My grandmother's heart melted when she looked at me, her anger subsiding as she gazed upon her youngest granddaughter, tiny and foreign; all her other grandkids were a decade older. She handed me a tin box covered by crochet that had bonbons inside. I opened the crochet-covered tin box and unwrapped the sweet cashew cream–filled candy as if I was taking communion. It was my favorite kind, wrapped in orange and red, called "Serenata de Amor," a serenade of love.

I suppose if I could eat a wish, that would be it: to be serenaded by love. Growing up with parents in different states spread the love thin. The simple pain of missing one and then the other is a heavy load for any little one, but add in living in different states, then different countries, feeling anger from one parent toward the other, and having little money and lots of stress, and you'll uncover the challenges millions of kids endure without lessons on how to do so.

Vovó grabbed a bottle of Johnny Walker Red out of the cabinet and poured my father a drink as he settled in by the TV, flipping the news on. She knew what made him happy. She used the old Johnny Walker Red bottles and glass Listerine bottles to keep chilled water in the fridge after carefully soaking them to remove the labels. The drinking water was "filtered" through a clay pot contraption that looked like it was from the 1930s, and though I didn't know it at the time, this pot was the cause of my yearly bouts of diarrhea and excruciating gut pain during my summer visits to Brazil with my dad. The pot didn't filter enough for my soft American belly. This yearly pain and purge became an annual emotional psychospiritual exorcism of sorts. It was one of the few places I could safely pour my upset into until I learned about booze, cigarettes, dieting, and other things that made the pain go away. At that time, though, life simply gave me the painful gift of releasing all the hurt into a ceramic toilet bowl with a water tank hanging overhead and a tiny chain I had to stand on my tiptoes to pull. In the States I had terrible belly aches, once getting so bad I had to go the hospital. When they did a scan at the hospital and stuck a tube down my throat, they saw two weeks of impacted bowels swelling around my stomach, which I now attribute to my fear of letting go and not feeling safe, so I was holding it all in. So in Brazil, although it was painful, I had a chance to be free of that, to release.

After I emptied my bowels into the beyond, I made my way back into the kitchen and poured myself another glass of water from the naked, smooth Listerine bottle in the 1950s fridge. I sipped slowly, wanting to rehydrate. I had no idea the water was actually what was poisoning me, so I kept going back to it. But as I learned later in life, one must drink poison at times to release; a poison with the power to sweep out the other poisons that are lodged in the body, mind, and spirit.

I sat down next to my grandma in the living room. She asked if I was okay, and I said yes, but her grandmotherly instincts knew better, and she said if I didn't get better, we would have to go to the doctor. I knew there was nothing else my family could do. Her hands crocheted quickly as she seemingly poured her fear and uncertainty into the threads. A statue of Mother Mary beamed at us from atop the TV.

My vovó Lourdes was born in 1919 in Ribeiraó Preto, Brazil. By the time I met her, her hair was bright silver and always neatly stacked atop her head in a perfect updo. Her skin was papery, and she wore silver bangles on her left wrist that matched her hair and jangled as she walked down the hallway of her tiny apartment. She had one silver bangle for each year she was married to my grandpa, vovô Bilá, who died quietly in his sleep from a heart attack when I was just four years old. My dad, the forever inappropriate jester, would always joke that he died after they made love one last time.

My grandmother's silver bangles stretched from her wrist to her elbow as a long piece of armor. She took them off only once a week for her bath, which was also the only time she took her hair down to comb and wash it. Otherwise, she was a symphony of constantly jangling silver everywhere she went, a metallic sound that brought comfort to my heart by simply reminding me she was there, my only anchor in a foreign world. She arrived at life's battles with fierceness, simplicity, sharpness, and shined beauty, at one point running a coffee and sugar cane plantation with grandpa while raising four kids and managing a tight household at the same time.

Her schedule was clear, strict, and orderly. I had no choice but to fall into it with her. It held both of us like a strong steel boat. A Capricorn matriarch, my grandmother was always regal and austere. She never showed emotion, but she was devoted to daily telenovelas full of emotion and drama that played every evening before dinner.

Her apartment was filled with plants, rows and rows of them by windows, and it had a humid smell that made me feel like we were in a jungle. Sometimes I'd press my face into them, lingering in their softness. I never asked her why she had so many plants, but perhaps it was her way of bringing her previous open-skied, lush farm life into her tiny city apartment.

Every morning, my grandma woke up at 7 am, did her daily stretches and exercises, and ate her breakfast of black coffee in a tiny cup, a plate of fruit that always included papaya, and a piece of bread. Then she went to her office, where she did "office things" that I didn't understand as a little girl. While she did that, I lazed around, thumbing through the Brazilian comic books my father bought me, the fashion magazine I got at the airport, and my journal. I remember looking out the window and watching the day pass while my stomach gurgled and grumbled.

One day, I was in particularly deep, gut-wrenching pain, having frequent bouts of diarrhea. My face was white, and I felt completely alone. I sipped the water from the clay pot and felt more grumbling in my belly. My grandmother was there, worried, but I was far from my mother and friends. My dad was away on a business trip, and I was left with her, simply going through the motions of our daily routine. I told her over and over that I was okay, but I wasn't. I didn't know how to tell her I was in pain. I tried to be good and not take up too much space, to hold it all together, but I could tell my grandma was worried because she expressed more emotion than I had ever seen her express. I heard her on the red plastic rotary phone in the other room, mumbling. She made several calls that day. I dozed off on the couch, feeling weak and disoriented. I didn't know how to ask for help. What would I even ask for? Someone to love me? Someone to save me? For my parents to be there when I needed them most? I had no words for the kind of help I needed, so I just held it all in.

A few hours later, the elevator dinged and several women arrived, white- and silver-headed, fat and thin, with spines that had begun to curve like bowing trees. They carried casseroles, loafs of banana bread, sweet treats, and cheese bread. The satellite TV with its bunny-ear antennae was turned on, and the Pope was giving mass in the Vatican as the silver-haired crones circled around.

Even though my dad made it clear that he was sexually abused by Catholic priests, my grandma could never abandon the Catholic church. I suppose if she'd chosen to believe him, she would have had to feel the guilt of sending him away to boarding school at age eight. I imagine she simply wasn't able to handle that reality. Somewhere inside, in the dark shadows, or tucked in an inner closet, she probably felt awful for his pain, but she could not let go of the Pope, the Virgin, or her rituals and prayers.

My grandmother came to get me from the twin bed I slept on in the back bedroom. I got up, weak, sad, and in pain. She asked me to step into the center of the circle of crones and lie on the floor. They lit candles, and the scent of rose soap, lavender cologne, and hairspray filled the room. The Pope gave his sermon, and then the screen turned to an image of Mother Mary as the words of the rosary scrolled across the screen. The sun had begun to set outside the windows of the apartment. I lay on the rug that covered the brown wall-to-wall carpet. I breathed slowly, my guts turning themselves in circles, pythons burrowing into a hole in the earth of my body. Like a kite that suddenly slips out of a hand, I flew up above my body to view the scene: a circle of silver and white crowns, with me lying in a fetal position in the center, a crocheted pillow under my head, and the humid, verdant plants witnessing the strange ritual.

The crones' voices droned a familiar mantra: "Ave-Maria, cheia de graça! O Senhor é convosco . . ." Like a circle of witches casting a spell on me, they incanted through the evening. Bony fingers ran over the smooth beads on their rosaries, their lips dry, their thin skin crackling, their thick ankles stuffed into nude pantyhose under long skirts. As the room grew darker, their words intensified, and tears began to stream down my face. I felt a wave of grace waft into the room, an indescribable feeling. My bowels unknotted themselves, and I felt no pain. Something in me softened. Was it the water that had poisoned me? Or was it my own pain?

When they finished reciting their words, they blew out the candles and turned on the lights. They fed me banana bread and sugary desserts made of guava and chocolate, then began chatting casually about the best way to reuse cooking grease and who had recently died. Meanwhile, I was still in a stupor of grace.

Soon after, the women shuffled out and said in Portuguese, "See you soon," to which my grandma responded, "God willing." Together, my grandmother and I watched telenovelas until it was time for bed, sipping chicken broth and not speaking of what had happened in the hours prior.

On that day, I felt what faith is. Their prayer to Mary has stayed with me until now. I call on her in dark times, when I am on my knees asking for mercy, when I am lying on the floor of my closet feeling despair. I pray the words of the rosary in Portuguese even though I am not Catholic. And when I went to Lourdes, France, I wept for Grandma Lourdes and her prayers for her American granddaughter. I wept for her human form that died at ninety-two with whispers of prayers upon her lips, and I held close her silver bangles that were dispersed among her children and that now live on my arm.

Emotional and physical pain can often be intertwined. The knots in the belly can be knots of pain that has simply never been felt. Not always, of course. But sometimes, yes. Sometimes all those emotions that had nowhere to go get stuck and churn into painful headaches and belly aches and cramps and backaches. Sometimes those places are a part of us asking for care, for healing, for love. Sometimes attention is the healer. Sitting with someone you love who can be fully present. **When we are present to our pain, it often starts to move.** But sometimes the pain is part of the gift. It carves a way in our being, it initiates us, it awakens us, calling us into the power of prayer, of ritual, of time. Our pain finally gets acknowledged, seen, and held, and has space to be set free.

Dare
to
Feel

REFLECTIONS

- Have you ever found yourself far from home, feeling alone and in pain? How old were you? Beneath any physical pain, was there something perhaps you were yearning for?

- How comfortable are you at being seen in your pain? Do you usually minimize the impact of pain on you or maximize it? Be honest and don't judge yourself.

- What is your relationship to the power of prayer and ritual, and how do these practices help you dare to feel?

- Have you had any experiences where feeling pain has awakened you to new truths about yourself or your situation?

RITUAL FOR OFFERING

Plan an outing to a place you consider sacred and make an offering there. This could be a religious place, even one you are not affiliated with but that you are free to visit. This could be a place in nature you hold sacred. It could be somewhere in your own yard. Bring flowers, incense, a candle, some oil or water, an offering for each of the five elements if you are outside. If you are going into a temple or chapel, bring a flower and light a candle there, and perhaps some incense if you can. Contemplate or pray and feel the grace and sacred tone of the space, whether it is the ocean, the tall trees around you, stained glass windows, or the scent of sandalwood in the air. Feel your connection to the mystery around you and offer your heart to it with a few words.

MY KIND OF WOMAN

The spiritual traditions I was raised in showed me woman
as virgin
and mother
and whore.

These were the options.

And then I looked elsewhere
because I knew there had to be more!

I saw a woman I aspired to be in
nature,
volcanos,
rosebuds,
forest fires,
the ocean.

A She who was fierce,
active,
dark,
and light—
pure power
meeting pure love!

Wild!
Ferocious!
Ecstatic!

I found Her in
a pregnant pause,
a flower blooming,
a last leaf falling.

The She in Me
was more than labels
and roles,
archetypes and ideas.

She was the rain,
a gust of wind,
a fire.

My kind of woman.

Courage and Curiosity
Bring Us Back into the Heart

If I was a teenager today, would I dare to feel? Or would I scroll on TikTok for hours, then pick up a video game controller and eat a bag of M&M's? Would I ace my homework like a mofo, work out like a pro, and let my perfectionism hold back all the feelings?

On the spectrum of dodging the discomfort of feeling, where do you fall? More M&M's or more work? More obvious or more covert? Obviously, there is a wide spectrum, but it is important to assess . . . when things get intense in life, how do you cope?

Overworking is a socially acceptable way to not feel, or not deal with, what's really happening inside. The more obvious ways many of us avoid feeling the deep or tough stuff are with sugar, booze, social media, and TV, but the less obvious ones involve overworking, caring so much for other people that we don't need to look at ourselves, or working on ourselves so much, but never stopping to really feel. This is a way we avoid living from depth. This is a way we avoid living from love. This is a way we avoid a deeper connection to Spirit.

If we stop to feel, would we have to come to terms with the shame and guilt of fully recognizing that most of us live on stolen land? That mostly immigrant labor fuels the USA, though many immigrants have been separated from their children and have very limited rights? That little ones are and have been stuck at the border in cages, treated like animals? If we stop to feel, would we have to look at where and how gas is made, and what resources are running out? What toxins are in our food and makeup and hair products? Would that feel scary to face for many of us? Exhausting? Overwhelming?

Would we have to stop and feel the pain of the voice inside that says, "You'll never be good enough"? Would we have to feel the shame of how we have dropped the ball on a friendship? Would we have to let the uncertainty of why we are here, and who or what created us, and what a miracle it is to be alive blow our minds a little bit? Would we have to stop and bow to this life we are amidst, humbled by the mystery?

From the personal to the political to the spiritual, there is so much to feel that it can be terribly overwhelming, and with that overwhelm, we often dare not to feel any of it. Most of us come from a culture of fast fixes, urgent care, Band-Aids, and Advil. But there is no bandage for unfelt emotional pain. Booze or TV can numb it for a while, but it will always return, knocking at the door to say, "Feel me!" But opening the door invites in a tidal wave, and what if you don't know how to surf? In that case, many of us believe it is better to keep the door closed and keep taping the edges so no water leaks in. But we know that one day the door will burst, and it will all come pouring out. Holding it at bay works only for so long because not feeling is actually more exhausting than the feeling part. It takes constant muscle to hold it down. It drains the color from your face and sucks your joy.

So even though the tidal wave of deep feeling is often frightening, it's necessary. And if you open it yourself, whether in therapy, with a teacher or a friend, in a meeting, or on a retreat, you can learn how to stay afloat in that sea of feelings. You can learn that the discomfort of feeling is no worse than the discomfort of a long workout. Wading through the sadness is indeed a heart workout! The shame will feel like a parade of fire ants under your skin that you can't run from. The rage will bubble volcanically, but you will not let it scald you, or take you under. Instead you'll channel it into writing and art and positive action, that, your heart will expand into a sea of compassion that it through humanity. **This is the path of a true heart warrior: ing all, letting it wash over you like a wave, and letting it** wake you up, bring you to your knees, make dewy drops in the corners of your eyes, and inspire you to raise your fists and stay open the whole damn time.

How do you make the leap from "I'm feeling anxious, I'm going to pick up my phone and scroll" to "I'm feeling anxious—I'm going to write, shake it out, contemplate what's under the anxiety, connect with a friend, journal about it, take some deep breaths, or just sit in the anxious muck"? To make that leap you first have to have the courage to be honest with yourself: "Wow, I've reached for my phone fifty times in the last hour. Interesting." Or, "Hmm I'm dreaming about a bottle of wine this evening and counting down the minutes till I get to have it. Curious!" Bearing nonjudgmental witness to the ways you avoid feeling is the first step. After that, the question is: "What is here? General stress? Too much busy? Fear about money? What am I avoiding, and what emotion comes with it? Guilt? Shame? Fear? Sadness? Anger? Joy? Tenderness?" We don't just feel discomfort at the seemingly "negative" sensations and emotions. We also often feel discomfort at FEELING GOOD! So there's that. We can be in a habit of constant worry or future tripping and actually be avoiding the present that surrounds us: a beautiful day with sun, sipping tea while reading outside. Relaxing into that scene of "feeling good" or "content" can itself be a feat as we may have to traverse guilt and shame that we have the privilege of free time and space to rest. It is complex the ways we block feeling ANY of it. Because there is so much swimming inside of each of us.

But do not let the volume of felt experience that each of us holds scare you. Instead, look at it like you have one million flavors inside, and you get to taste them all in this life! Or you can stay content with the three flavors you know. If you cultivate curiosity and if you know that each emotion and sensation will end eventually, like a ride at the fair, could you have the courage to surrender a little more deeply into it? And if you are one of those people who, if you surrender deeply to it, may never get off the ride, then set a timer, plan an activity, create structure so you don't stay always drifting in the inner seas but you also put your love in action.

That is part of the magic of opening your heart wide again after it's been hurt and trampled on and broken and violated . . . when you do start to trust and feel again, you can't help but be inspired to TAKE ACTION. To give, to serve, to inspire. It may take a minute, sure. A closed heart that doesn't want to feel the ick or yum can take time to coax back into the arena of life. But when you feel into the world and all the beauty and chaos, if you deeply feel it, how could you live a life of simply watching TV or scrolling? Something in you will awaken. You will want to pour your heart into something. It doesn't have to be political or activism or social change, but maybe it is! It could also be creative, it could be personal, it could be simply showing up as a better friend. It can be a deep spiritual commitment to your life. **Feeling our emotions connects us to the deepest levels of humanity that we are a part of, and that creates a deeper invitation into living life fully alive.**

Dare *to* Feel

REFLECTIONS

- When things get intense, how do you cope? What is the first sign you have lost connection to yourself and life?

- When do you unconsciously choose to disconnect, and why? What is the threshold of pain or discomfort that has you jump ship from staying connected to the moment?

- What states are the most unbearable for you? What do you resist? What do you lean into?

- Do you think it is possible to stop judging yourself and start being curious about why? What would you have to give up in order to do that?

- Where and when do you feel too sensitive for this world and need to hide and numb?

- What intention could help you commit to staying open to life and in your heart, even when it hurts?

RITUAL FOR INSPIRED ACTION

Select a day when you set an intention to choose inspired action instead of your usual coping mechanisms. Some ideas for inspired action are: praying, dancing, moving fear or anxiety through the body in breath, having a big cry, sitting in meditation, baking something for someone you love, and writing your heart out. Let the whole day be a ritual of commitment to not reaching for the quick fix, but instead asking yourself to be with what is. Pour that energy into each inspired action that you take.

A PRAYER OF AMENDS TO LIFE

Life, I owe you an apology.

I've been casual about the gifts you have given me,
and I'm embarrassed.

I've been lazy.

I've had my head in my phone and have missed your sunsets.

I've heard the call to help the animals
and the children
and the elderly,
as I did in my youth,
but I haven't taken action.

I've been too busy to watch the turning of your leaves.
I've been too caught up with my worries
to celebrate my orgasmic potential.
I've forgotten the beauty in each tear.
I've missed the joy of a simple rain.
It is time to make amends.

It is time to promise I won't let life fly by
while lost in my phone,
lost in worry,
lost in thought.

So here I am,
bowing before you
instead of bowing before my devices.

Asking you for mercy.
Asking, "Is there still time?"

Asking for your compassion,
asking for your aid.

Please wake me when I am asleep.
Shock me when I have forgotten.
Help me stay present here in this realm.

Because my everything depends on it.
Thank you, thank you, thank you.

PART 2

OPENING THE HEART AGAIN AFTER DIVING INTO ITS SHADOWS

Courage to Face
Our Core Wounds

I t may seem like life gets more intense as we look into our most tender, closed, or hurt places, the places longing to be felt, healed, and called forth into our hearts. When I say *healed*, I mean that some aspect of your being has been brought into consciousness, out of the shadowlands of denial or repression or shame, illuminating unconscious reactions, behaviors, and lived, repeated stories. I mean entering a conscious state of awareness where choices can be made and nothing has to be hidden. To me, healing is living from choice, moment to moment, instead of existing on autopilot reactions that were imprinted by societal or familial conditioning, or defenses, or as reactions to hurt. **Healing occurs when the bridge between you and your most essential self, your soul, is restored.** It is a rejoining of the fractured you with the Whole You, and it can happen in one thousand ways, again and again and again.

If you are more than ready to live from the heart, some repairs may need to be done first before you begin to open. You may first need to feel and heal some of the deepest, toughest mind-body-soul stuff buried within you, and liberate yourself from its invisible vice grip around your throat. When you ask for that to be moved and cleared, a lot can, and will, arise to be *felt* first. This arising can feel excruciating or overwhelming or cathartic, or all of these at once. And if it's you want for yourself, you may attract the exact medicine the hurts buried within you, in life circumstances and r until whatever needs to come up to be felt and cleared has the space to do so. This is the transformational path of the heart.

Some people try to heal by *avoiding* walking straight into the scary places of their being. Some might even think, *Well, I would prefer to stay away from this, or that, because it brings up a lot for me.* But the bringing up, tenderly, is often the exact thing that heals you. This is an ancient notion found in the depths of many spiritual traditions and philosophies.

We must first turn toward the feelings and experiences that are stuck within us, causing us pain and closing our hearts. Some of this wounding and pain may have been passed down from generation to generation, and to get into it we need to acknowledge our ancestors and get curious about their stories, their rituals, and their traditions. We also have to stop and get clear about and acknowledge what pain or patterns are there before any healing or transformation can occur. And this is why we repeat patterns, because we often try so hard to heal a thing without actually addressing it, and until it is truly acknowledged, loved, and healed, it will keep living as a behavior or pattern that causes discomfort. For example, when I feel abandoned (even if I am not truly being abandoned but simply feel the threat), the pain of my childhood abandonment arises. I often do not want to feel all of that, so as a coping mechanism, I try and construct a life where no one can abandon me. I can look back into my lineage and see that my father carries a big abandonment wound that was passed on to me. I can look into the strategy of coping with life's pain and stress with alcohol that runs through the men in my family, and the buried dreams that the women lived with. These are simply a few surface-layer, obvious examples of patterns and wounds that are passed down. Some are less obvious. And some are new and unique to you and perhaps don't relate to your family directly.

Whatever pains or wounds we bury turn into habitual behaviors that eventually become deep-rooted patterns. Some people attempt to bury their pain by overworking, overusing social media, drinking, watching television, or even by engaging in spiritual practice (very common in many circles!). In these instances, the emotions and sensations trying to rise up and be healed don't have space to do so. If these challenges are never addressed, and are avoided throughout a lifetime, I believe the soul will have to return to this planet to try and heal again, because there is no escaping the path. For the souls who have made vows to heal and burn through as much karma as possible in this life, this awakening road may be thick and deep and take massive courage.

The emotions, sensations, and inner voices that say, "This is too much! I can't handle this!" often become louder and louder as we get closer and closer to healing something. Deep inside, the abandoned, rejected, or scared version of ourselves awaits with its walls of protection. As the pain gets triggered, the walls come up, and as we get closer to healing, they get fiercer and louder. This is where most people give up. They leave the relationship, the job, or the dream they tried to make come true because it is "too hard." But the wound inside is also too hard to live with. The buried thing, be it deep shame, guilt, or abandonment, is also too hard to carry for a lifetime, too hard to avoid all the people and moments that could trigger it.

So ask yourself: "How many lifetimes will I spend avoiding my deepest wound?" There are no shortcuts in healing, only helpers along the way, like meditation, prayer, chanting, sacred plants, song and dance, time in nature, and soul friends. Over time, a soul learns how to stand with grace, even amidst the greatest fires and pains that arise from the past.

For someone not on the path of soul awakening, this all may sound very silly! Why call forth your deepest pains, traumas, and fears? Why knock on those closed doors? Why disturb the things we have buried?

Because that is the way to awaken.

To open the doors.

To disrupt the sleeping corpses.

To let the light in.

To air it all out.

To grasp this, we must relinquish our yearning to "be right" and forgo our old stories and self-righteousness. We must look at the places that hurt, the places that are embedded in the psychospiritual-emotional realms, the landmines inside, the buried pains, the deepest core wounds. **We must have courage to take the time to shift the focus from blame to self-responsibility, which liberates us into our own healing.**

We either construct a life around avoiding this healing, or we construct a life around getting to know the closed or hardened places in our beings, opening them up, staring straight into them, and trusting and loving the path we are on. Seeing that underneath some of the emotions that arise, there is always a gift awaiting us. And this is where living from the heart begins. **When we have the courage to dig deep and be with what is, and then stay open and live open, we dare to walk the transformational path of the heart.**

Dare *to* Feel

REFLECTIONS

- What coping mechanisms are favored in your family, and how are these reflected in your own coping strategies in the face of discomfort?

- How are hard feelings approached within your family? Can you think of any examples that illustrate this?

- How do your family members acknowledge trauma within the family? How is it dealt with?

- What is your belief system around karma or the soul's journey—the notion that there is a bigger story at play that your soul opted into? How would it feel to talk about this idea with your family? Do your beliefs in this area differ from those of the family you grew up within?

- What would you consider some of your core wounds, and how have these impacted your capacity for deep feeling? (Some examples: Guilt, shame, rejection, denial, abandonment, repression, fear of being alone, fear of speaking up.)

RITUAL FOR ANCESTRAL RECLAIMING

Get curious about how your ancient ancestors used to practice grieving or feeling rage or going through life's transitions before the advent of organized religion. Did they engage in ceremonial or ritualistic songs or dances? Communion with nature? Ritual with the moon? A particular type of cleansing ritual? Do some research and see if you can incorporate one element of their practices into your life today. See if you can source into a time when humans didn't have all the coping mechanisms we do now, and instead had rituals, songs, and rites of passage. Use this as a way of honoring any pain, discomfort, and deep or overwhelming feelings when they arise.

NOT FOR THE FAINT OF HEART

The healing journey is not for the faint of Heart.

To feel the highs and lows
of humanity through the magic portal
of your physical being?

Ooh la la!

They come like waves,
volcanic eruptions
that shake you sometimes,
tickle you at others,
mend your wounds,
and then throw salt in them to see where it still hurts.

Oh, this journey!

We don't know when we will arrive somewhere new,
or when we will be taken by the eruption . . .

When it comes, it is sometimes like a slap in the face,
a punch in the gut
that takes away your breath!

It asks you to stand and face
the invisible opponent . . .

Which is Your Brilliant Healing Journey.

Which is You,
a new you,
whole and true.

Yearning and Learning to Feel Safe

By age twenty-one, I was fully committed to my spiritual path, to living on the fringe outside of the mainstream, close to the Goddess, my moon blood, the moon, and the invisible realms. I had begun to feel again, to open my heart to life, and to let myself be held by community and cultures that honored the earth and our spiritual lives as humans. It was 2006, and I had just returned from Italy, where I learned meditation and sat in caves on hard rocks with young yogis, praying and chanting for hours. I had begun to find my own blend of Eastern spiritual paths, plus a more earth-based pagan side of myself close to the Goddess. The Rainbow Gathering, an unofficial festival in the woods full of workshops, parties, yoga, and ritual, seemed like it would have room for all of me. My heart was hungry for connection as it started awakening and peeping out from behind the walls I had built to keep me safe.

The night before my best friend Rebecca and I left for the gathering, we moved out of our South Park Slope apartment. I drank too much red wine and played my accordion on the fire escape that faced the inside of the building, with all its windows protecting the homes of sleeping children and mostly Latin families. There I was, drunkenly freestyling new songs on my accordion, a wild, free woman. I should've been a little embarrassed and more self-aware, but I was not, and that was that. I had just graduated college, and it felt like my life was really beginning.

Rebecca and I packed two small bags and a little tent for the festival. As far as we knew, food and other amenities would be provided. This was just as well, as I was in thousands of dollars of student loan debt. I was also on Medicare and had an EBT card that afforded me with $200 worth of groceries a month. A gal like me wasn't supposed to end up in NYC. I didn't come from money, but I had hustled to get there and stay there as my soul sensed the liberation the place would provide me, something very different than my Marietta, Georgia, life. I also had a small flip phone at the time that didn't work in the middle of nowhere, and texting still wasn't as big of a thing as it is today. With no such thing as Google Maps for support, we knew we would have to stop and ask for help if we got lost.

We arrived to the Rainbow Gathering in a car full of deodorant-less Brooklyn hippie gals, our Subaru packed to the brim with our bags and blankets and tents and coolers. We lined up to get "in" to the outdoor, unfenced gathering among hordes of other hippies, gutter punks, Hare Krishna followers, and festivalgoers and soon found a place to camp, noticing a lot of empty space among red oak, beech, maple, and birch trees. It was quiet and peaceful, and we were thankful there weren't a ton of people where we were setting up. We set up our tent and left our backpacks in it, heading out to explore with just a small satchel of the important things.

My uniform of choice included a long white skirt and black lace-up leather boots that I got in Italy when my mom came to visit for a week, a week I spent in shock. Just six months prior, I had gone to Prague, wide-eyed and naïve, trusting, and a bit reckless, and had ended up being date raped. Of course, like many women do, I blamed myself. I went into such a state of shock and self-shame that I didn't speak to my mom much the whole trip. I couldn't let her in, but she bought me the boots as a token of her love. They meant something to me, proof that somebody loved me, even when I was in a deep freeze from trauma I didn't know how to face.

At that tender age, I was still individuating from my parents, still trying to forgive and make peace with my father, who felt like an alien to me. I was trying to become un-enmeshed with my mother, who felt like a sister to me. Every psychic I've seen in my life has told me my mother and I have lived lifetimes together, and that it is big karma for her to be my mother this time around. But I tried my hardest not to be her big sister; I tried to break free. So, there I was, completely untethered from her, and really from anyone besides Rebecca, in the West Virginia forest.

This made me cling to Rebecca a bit as we walked around the festival grounds, encountering chai tea camps, African dance classes, drum circles, and yoga groups. She was older than me and much more confident. The Aquarius to my Pisces. I was at a tender point in my journey and often felt emotionally naked. I could feel everything in every room I entered; I was a skilled energetic tracker, a skill born of trauma. Hypervigilance kept me removed from the moment, always two steps ahead anticipating danger, noticing every detail around me. (This skill only turned off with the consumption of alcohol, something I learned brought a sense of relief from the constant vigilance, and also blindness to true dangers.) This hypervigilance also meant my energetic boundaries were porous, and that I always heard every sound in a dark room and sensed things coming before they happened. I was always tracking what sound was what in the dark, what person was trustable or not, and where the nearest exit was. Because as a kid I didn't always feel like my parents were tracking me and my needs and safety, I learned how to do it myself.

At the Rainbow Gathering, sleeping in the woods and with no cell service, I sensed myself meeting edges around feeling safe in my body. I was curious if I would meet a lover or kindred spirit there, which I felt could help me feel more at ease, as I seemed to always be on the hunt for one. We hadn't brought alcohol with us on the journey, and it wasn't a place I would want to drink, among thousands of people. Having some wine in my home with friends felt safe, but here I vowed to stay sober and alert.

That first night, we quickly realized why there was so mu at our camp site: our tent was right next to the medic cam people typically went if they had had a bad trip! I laid awake while Rebecca snored next to me and a man outside yelled, "I HAVE THE BIG-GEST MOTHERFUCKING DICK!" This went on all night long. At first it was comical, but it quickly became frightening. Ten years later, when Rebecca insisted that I go to Burning Man with her, I brought ear plugs, a white noise machine, an air mattress, a down comforter, and sweet twinkling lights to make my tent feel more like home. But that night, in the middle of the woods at the Rainbow Gathering, I had none of that, not even a head lamp or a sleeping mat.

As the week unfolded, we accepted the fact that sleeping next to the medic camp was going to be rough, as was the daily search for food. I imagined there would be camps of happy hippies everywhere serving stew, with gentle sunrise chimes and fragrant sage wafting through the air while mantras were chanted. But it was not quite like that. One morning, in an attempt to get some grub, we wandered into a camp of drunken middle-aged men who were making eggs and drinking cans of Bud at 8 am, rumbling, shirtless, some toothless, with a fierce stench. My happy hippie kumbaya fantasy of the Rainbow Gathering melted like faded tie dye during a bad trip.

The bathroom situation was even more adventurous. There were no porta potties, just thousands of people relieving themselves in giant troughs in the forest. Sometimes lanterns lit the way, and some of the restroom areas were magical, mossy little spots. But all in all, there were no doors, and often you had to go while other strangers did their business next to you. This was an edge I had never faced. I had pooped in Brazil and Mexico in small, strange bathrooms, some with no run-ning water. I had pooped with a friend in the bathroom with me. But I had never released my waste, or deeply let go of anything, with that many people around. It brought up a primal fear and shame. It was the one thing I had been taught to keep private my whole life. My guts, my belly, what I rid myself of daily. It felt too vulnerable for me to share it with strangers.

So for five days, I couldn't poop. On the sixth morning, I walked into the forest determined to do it. I hitched up my skirt and squatted.

Days' worth of Hare Krishna curry was backed up in my guts, and I prayed for sweet release. As I began to breathe into relaxation, a gray-haired, middle-aged, hippie guy dropped his pants just a few feet away. I tried to steady myself and stay the course, but I couldn't do it. As I heard his feces drop into the trough, I met my own spiritual edge. I may have been free, but clearly I was not *that* free.

Over the rest of the week, my discomfort deepened. I tried to go off on my own into the woods from time to time, and I managed a little here and there, but essentially I did not poop for an entire week. My body felt too unsafe to relax and let go, a pattern I had been repeating from childhood. Any time I was on guard or felt unsafe as a kid, I would get constipated and refuse to open and relax. The Rainbow Gathering was a place where all were welcome to be free and be themselves; it was technically a "safe space" where people gathered in the name of peace. But it was still an unregulated space in the middle of the woods with thousands of people, some of whom were on lots of drugs. And though in theory it was a "safe space," I did not feel safe at my core.

This trip also offered me an opportunity to awaken to my empathetic gifts and know and accept that I was very open and therefore needed actual safe spaces to be held by. The experience of sexual trauma I had been through just a few months back was in me, and on some level I was still healing from the experience of trusting a stranger and having it turn out nightmarishly. I had my spiritual path and practice, but I still heavily guarded my female body, and my heart. I was slowly learning to walk through life with an open heart while also having boundaries and letting myself be held by life. I vacillated between total surrender and blind trust and being closed off and guarded, still seeking a middle ground.

One day, Rebecca suggested she and I do our own thing. I imagined she needed space to be confident and free in a way that I was not, so I spent the day talking to some yogis at the Hare Krishna camp, watching a children's puppet show, and sitting by a drum circle in a big field. As the sun set, I wandered into the dark. I stood around a bonfire as people danced and spun fire. It did not occur to me then that most people were on drugs. There was clearly alcohol everywhere though, and some people were passed out. I walked back to the areas surrounding our camp. It felt safer there, with the trees creating a haven and the madness of the bigger parties melting into the distance.

I wandered a bit, breathing deeply and holding my tiny flashlight with nowhere to go. I thought, *Should I just go back to our tent? Am I that shy and awkward?* I looked for another edge to meet and saw a camp that looked inviting. Though I was tired of meeting edges at that point, I decided to go in. There was live guitar music, popcorn, a makeshift treehouse, and another campfire with people chatting around it. It felt safe, like a warm relief from my solitary walk in the big, dark forest in the name of my spiritual growth. I sat down next to some folks who were chatting and shyly said hello. I ended up speaking to a guy in a little black felt fairy hat who was jovial, nonthreatening, and kind.

"You're from Georgia?!" he exclaimed. "You must go to Hostel in the Forest! It is a magical land in the middle of the swamp, and you will love it. If you needed a message about where to go, this is it!"

Even though I felt tentative about letting strangers in, that small moment at the cozy campsite allowed me to open up and feel. The people there were lucid, sober, and alert, their eyes twinkling under the lights. The music felt good in my body, and the crowd felt welcoming and conscious. My nervous system relaxed there, and I enjoyed the music for a while before wandering back to our tent to sleep. I made it back before Rebecca, but I felt complete. I learned more about myself that night. Yes, I was always tracking what was safe or unsafe. Perhaps I felt closed off or unapproachable because I kept my guard up until I felt safe, but when I did feel safe I knew how to let my guard down. I didn't need alcohol to force my guard down in moments when I didn't actually feel good or safe. It was better to be patient with my sweet heart and accept myself as is. Perhaps I wasn't the one who would wander and talk to strangers in the dark. Perhaps I was the gal who would sit by the small campfire with the popcorn, close to home. And that was okay.

The next morning, I walked into the woods by our camp. Mist mingled with the leaves, and little sun rays began to spill onto the earth. It was early, and there was peace in the lack of noise. Dew kissed everything, making it all gleam. There was no one else around, so I hitched up my skirt and squatted by the trough. I was in mid-release when a dreadlocked woman in a patchwork, open-back dress wandered up with her two little ones. She smiled at me, then turned away, helping her kids and honoring my privacy as best as she could. The littles chatted and she talked back, which made the perfect sound buffer. Though they were about six feet away, I was finally able to let go.

A month later, I still remembered the man in the black fairy hat, and I made it a point to go to Hostel in the Forest. There I felt completely safe and held. I could open my heart and connect with new people, and it felt safe. I swam in the lake naked every day, ventured into my first sweat lodge, made love to a man with a snake tattoo that traveled up his spine, and circled with a motley crew of wild and free spirits and travelers for dinner every night. I felt at home there, with its communal dinners, compost toilets, and mosquitoes that nipped at me as I relieved myself in peace and private with ease. I felt at home among a smaller group of people who had a shared vision in how they viewed spirit and life. The swamp of Georgia, with its relentless humidity and draping Spanish moss, felt like home in some way.

Feeling safe or unsafe determines so much for us. We can often push through not feeling safe, but the body doesn't lie. If the body doesn't feel safe, it will not poop. It will not orgasm. Even though you may be telling yourself, "This is safe!" there is nothing you can say or do if your body doesn't feel it. There may be old stuff keeping you from feeling safe, or new ways to meet reality that you are learning. You may also be reckoning with the truth that some things that feel safe for others don't feel safe for you. And that is okay! You must not compare yourself to the other people around you, because their life experiences likely have been so different from yours. Your journey of feeling safe to open up to new people, to let your body relax, and to disarm your fears is your own. No one can speed that up for you or tell you to get over it. This is where you must be fierce with your own self-loving and have compassion for anyone who tries to rush you past your edges. And yet, also, you must be brave so you don't let the patterns born from hurt dictate your whole life. Meeting your edges with kindness and compassion will change the patterns over time. Being curious as to what is true for you, and what is a choice from fear, is discernment that takes time to cultivate.

The Rainbow Gathering revealed that I had a lot of healing to do around trusting men, and at the root of my anxiety was mostly a fear of men that started with my childhood. I had to work on that for many years thereafter. Sleeping in a tent at a festival of thousands didn't feel safe to me, nor did dropping my panties in public, even if I was just pooping like everyone else.

No matter the pain or trauma that is causing you to not feel, or to feel too much, know that it can be faced, loved, and not forced to change but rather invited to change with love. Our bodies tell so much of the story of our soul's lessons and victories. We cannot ignore them. They are precious and wise. This is where we get curious, we get compassionate, we practice patience. If we want to overcome the patterns in our body, we have to see that it will take time, but that it is possible. We can also get curious about what does feel right or safe. When does it feel GREAT to open? What moments bring you into deep relaxation? When do you let your guards down? By noticing those moments, too, you can begin to bring awareness to how you could create trust and safety in the moments when you don't want to open.

Life will inevitably be scary. But we cannot wait to open our hearts and enjoy life until all the circumstances are perfect. That will never happen. We can do our best to hold our sweet hearts, and the little ones inside us, and yet to take strides in taking risks and retraining ourselves to feel safe in moments when the habit is to not feel safe. This can be as simple as telling a friend, "This is a HUGE edge for me to go to this party where I don't know anyone, but I am excited to do it. I am wondering if we could have an hourly check-in and meeting point. Would you be down for that?" It will be vulnerable to ask for what would help you feel safe, but I imagine likely you will be met with love and compassion from those who care about you. And if you take a risk and can't do it and need to go home and cry, that is okay, too. This is how we heal. We don't hide from the fears; we meet them head on, with kindness and care. The journey to openness and healing is humbling. Hold yourself tenderly as you courageously walk toward it.

Dare *to* Feel

REFLECTIONS

- In what locations do you feel safest in your body?

- With whom do you feel safest in your body?

- What does "safety" feel like to you? (For example: like a strong hand on my lower back; like I can breathe deeply)

- Where or when have you taken a risk on something unsafe and not been able to go through with it? What held you back? (Be kind to yourself here and acknowledge the fact that you even tried.)

- Where or when have you gone through with something unsafe and come away feeling braver than before? What helped you take this risk in the moment?

RITUAL FOR APPRECIATING COURAGEOUS RISK

Plan to take an hour outside in your own garden or in a local botanical garden, or walk through the flower garden of a friend or neighbor. On your walk, find a plant or tree to connect with; stroke or cup a plant with your hands, or sit with your back against a tree. You can also connect energetically to a plant or tree by closing your eyes and simply trying to feel. This ritual is best done in the spring! But if it is the middle of the winter, feel free to use your imagination and sit by a houseplant or a flower in a vase. Meditate on the journey of this plant. Imagine it as a seed flying through the air, and visualize how it grew its roots under the soil and eventually became a green shoot that pushed through the earth to become what it is now. Speak to the tree or plant or flower and praise its courage. See the plant as you, and see your own courage, too. Feel free to tend to it, water it, and make a relationship with it, seeing it as a sacred mirror of you.

LIVING OUTSIDE OF THE LIE

You make a face of disgust
when you must!
And it is a gift to all around you
to see that you do not agree
with whatever circus is playing out.

To agree would be to comply,
and you cannot!

Or your body will moan at you,
clench its fists,
and the heart will throb madly!

Living outside of the lie can feel lonely . . .
until you discover the others
who have also left!

And together you sit for tea,
letting your face be senseless and without a mask,
sounding the animal sounds of your pain,
crying the ugly tears of your deepest woe,
and laughing the cackling laughs at the absurdity of it all.

It can get messy here
with all these feelings,
but outside of the lie is Truth.

And your body knows Truth.

It feels like home.

So go there!

Be brave!

Let the lie go and find your way home.

Trying to Avoid Our Core Wounds but Falling Straight into Their Healing

For most of my life I tried at all costs to avoid dating anyone like my dad. It was a method I employed to avoid the pain and rage I felt toward strong, dominant men and the patriarchy in general. It was an excuse to keep myself in control. Did you know that you don't have to feel the vulnerable, sweet surrender of love if you are the one "in power"? Perhaps you'll feel it eventually, but you'll at least feel more in control along the way. But for me, I could not escape this curriculum of healing, as you likely cannot escape the curriculum your soul has set out for you. Life wanted me to get close to the tender spots in my deepest being, and I couldn't avoid the magnetic pull toward my own soul work. Life is smart like that. She always gets her way, and she always finds you, sometimes in a way you least expect. So, my first outside-of-my-control love that made me weak in the knees, that helped me to surrender to someone else's lead, came in the body of a woman. I had a deep, unconscious thought somewhere in the vault of my being that said, "This can't touch on my daddy issues. She's a *woman* . . ."

If we are here to do the soul work, it's pretty hard to avoid even if we try. And if we try, life gets crafty as to how it brings the soul lessons in.

I was in Brooklyn, walking around the music video set where I was a producer, when Gabriella, a production assistant, stared straight into my soul in a terribly disarming way. Her eyes lingered too long each time I asked her to grab something for me. I wore gray cotton leggings, Frye boots, and a pink vintage cardigan with a tank top underneath. My hair was a frizzy mess, and I didn't wear makeup at the time. I was focused on becoming a filmmaker, a real artist, and there was no space for frivolity, or so I thought. I assisted on film sets and produced small indie projects, inhabiting settings in which people passionately told their stories and were determined to get their work out into the world, all while I wrote my own scripts and hustled with multiple jobs to get by.

We were behind schedule on set that particular day, and I needed to go to the bank to get cash for a payment. I looked to the other producer, Tal, who said, "Gabriella can take you." I nodded and got into her car. Immediately, Gabriella stared straight into me with a look that said, "I see you," and I let her. At age twenty-five, I was still deeply searching for love, and for truth, everywhere I went.

I later found out that when Gabriella and I met, she had recently been cheated on and left by her ex, a leggy femme fatale with breasts that spilled out into every room and heels that resembled weapons. In hindsight, it's hard for me not to see Gabriella's hunger for me as a desire for revenge, but it didn't matter at the time. I was in a stifling relationship that looked really good on paper but that asked me to abandon my own needs daily. Gabriella's eyes promised liberation and acceptance into a world I had yet to enter: a world where I could be loved for who I was.

She drove us over the Brooklyn Bridge to a bank in lower Manhattan. The entire time, she asked about who I was and what I liked. It felt like she was already inside my chest, and it was frightening. I had a boyfriend, but my heart expanded like a hot air balloon of lust, confusion, intrigue, fear, and excitement in the car. By the time I got back to the set, I was stunned. *WTF was that?* I'm not sure I knew what it felt like to be seen that deeply and to feel fully held by someone's attention. It was new and beautiful.

A few months later, I was hers. She would not have taken no for an answer. She had conquered me and rescued me from the land of my ex-boyfriend, whom I had planned to move in with. In a flash, my life had been turned upside down. She showed me a queer, accepting community of people who loved to laugh and dance, and she said, "Come home. Come." I looked back and saw the world I was leaving, then turned my attention toward the Pride parade I was walking into and wept. I had never felt such love and belonging.

She was the first partner to carry my groceries, open every door for me, and use her body as a barrier between me and traffic on the crazy streets of NYC. I was safe! Finally! On the flip side, she also requested I wear a push-up bra, more makeup, lingerie, and . . . heels! I only wore heels to art openings or film festivals, and I always took cabs so I wouldn't have to walk in them. With Gabriella, I was asked to walk in Manhattan in heels. It was a leap for me, as was the push-up bra, which I hadn't worn since middle school because, well, I was a feminist, especially in my twenties. But I also recognized that we were taking those aspects of the patriarchy and playing with them, reappropriating them and having fun with them. A push-up bra was perhaps no longer oppressive when it was called in as an object of desire between two queer women. At least, that's what I told myself at first. My butch-femme dynamic with Gabriella required a lot from me when it came to dressing "feminine," but for the first time since living with my father, I sank into the dominating masculine lead of another, and felt held.

With Gabriella I could let go, and I often cried in her arms. I could be a hot mess and she would just look at me with a sly smile and say, "You done yet, baby? Come here." She knew how to melt me. From the day we met, my knees went weak in her presence. I relaxed into her. So when she broke up with me one year and seven months into our relationship, it felt like a car had crashed into my heart. My safe masculine presence was suddenly gone.

Right before the holidays, in my Greenpoint, Brooklyn, apartment, I laid in my bed, broken. In a flash I had lost everything—the promised land of community, future plans, ecstatic nights out dancing, Sunday mornings lounging on the couch, laughter, and passionate love making. It was all gone, and I was in shock. The sky was gray and thick, a gloomy winter haze of freezing wind blasting through naked trees. Everyone was in the process of making Christmas plans, and I was supposed to be with her and her family, the family that had taken me in. The family I now didn't have. We were supposed to have Christmas in Manhattan, chic yet relaxed, on the Upper West Side, where we would've had intellectual conversations at dinner, where she would've wrapped her arms around me. Where we would've come home and taken walks in the snow and talked about the sites we wanted to see in Hawaii for our friend's wedding happening over New Year's. But now it was all gone, and I was in shock. I'd dared to feel at home with her and her family. Because I didn't have a solid family unit of my own, I'd dared to let them in, to let them love me and see me. I lost her, my masculine rock, and I lost them, and the dream of what love could mean. There would be no more lobster boils in Hampton Bays on the Fourth of July, no more witty discourse over cocktails. It was all gone.

The pain of losing love is like no other, but it is not fully true. The truth is that Love doesn't ever really leave. The mirrors or the on-ramps to Love can vanish quickly, but Love itself stays with you, sitting beside you and reminding you that it is there. But too often we associate Love with a particular human, which is right and true, yet we believe the lie that this one person is the key to Love. In truth, they just show us what we already have inside.

A few months later, a psychic told me that the pain I felt wasn't about Gabriella, but rather it was about what had happened when my parents divorced when I was a kid: Mom and I left Dad, and I lost his masculine protection and love. She said I was just now able to feel that pain, and that my love for Gabriella was a necessary catalyst for having the space to feel what I went through when I was five, when I didn't have the skills to truly feel.

There I was at age twenty-six, finally able to feel it.

The loss hit me again and again. I would wake thinking, *Was it all a dream?* And it wasn't. I was still in the cold, gray winter of New York, and I was still heartbroken. I couldn't watch *TV*; I was in so much pain! *That* was a first. My friends Emma and Alyson came and sat on my bed in the dark as I laid there. They tried to get me to eat, but

I wouldn't. I was in a deep ceremony, revisiting the depth of my core wound, without many tools at the time, or guides.

I had lost Dad when I was a kid, and in Gabriella, I had gained a masculine force that felt so damn good. It had come in a way I could receive. She wasn't a macho dude I could write off; instead she was a strong, capable woman. That was life saying, "You can't run from this deep hunger to surrender into the love of another. You cannot stay in control when it comes to love. You will feel what it was like to be held by a loving masculine force, and then you will feel the loss, and you will heal." In that loss, I realized I needed that type of nourishment, no matter what body it came in. It was a hunger I was finally fully claiming after pushing it aside for so many years.

As I mourned our relationship, I barely ate; instead I eased my hunger by looking for that masculine force I so yearned for. I was hungry for more of that feeling. Sometimes I found it; other times I just found lust, sex, hangovers, and walks of shame. It was a dark time in many ways, and I walked into the realms of hungry ghosts in my own heart. I dated like a love-hungry monster trying to get its fix until I realized there was a masculine force *within me* that needed healing. And I didn't need anyone for that. That is the magic. That is where the path is winding and where it surprises you. Characters come and go from our soul's journeys with the unspoken contract of initiating us into something we have come for in this lifetime. We cannot attach the importance of a lesson or a feeling to a person; we simply must thank them for delivering the message, the lesson, the gift. And then we must let them go.

The lessons our soul is craving, the lessons that will help us open these hearts and minds up to life, will come whether we are willing to receive them or not. If we are unwilling to receive them, they may get louder and louder until there is no way we can say no to their healing gifts. But if we say yes to the people and situations that bump against our tender wounds and keep our eyes open, knowing we are healing, then it doesn't have to be a healing that sideswipes us but one we are fully aware of, fully participating with, and saying yes to.

Dare *to* Feel

REFLECTIONS

- Contemplate your surprise life lessons. In what moments have you learned something about yourself or the world that you didn't see coming, and what feelings accompanied this?

- Looking back on your life, what has been your greatest heartbreak? What imprint did it leave, and how did it change the way you love?

- Has there been a person in your life who helped you dare to feel? What was the feeling you got from being with that person? Where do you experience that feeling in your body?

- What is your relationship with internal archetypes? Can you feel an internal King or Daddy archetype as a part of your inner world and psyche? A part of you inside that takes protective care of yourself like a father? Feeling into the different aspects of you, using your imagination, consider what that internal masculine figure is like for you. When does that aspect of fatherly support emerge?

RITUAL FOR CELEBRATING LOVE

Sit and create your ritual space. Get a pen and a piece of paper. Write a poem about your greatest loves in honor of each person whom you have loved (romantically or platonically) and who has loved you back. It can be long or short. Do not worry if it is "good" or if it makes sense. While you write, feel the love in your heart emerge. Perhaps add some details about these loved ones, nods to certain memories, scents, or songs. Feel the celebration and also the longing that may arise. Let your heart be enlivened by the love you have experienced. Carry the poem with you, and when you feel called, set it free into the sea or down a river, saying "thank you" all the while, and daring to feel the love and gratitude that is eternal.

LOVE UNSAFE

Loving with a fully open heart is so vulnerable.

There is zero safety net.

It means being so open,
it means being so generous,
it means risking everything.

But loving in a way that feels safe
and chill
and controlled
is not the love that you truly yearn for,
is it?

You want a love that moves like nature's fury
and like miracles in motion!

You want the kind of loving that is completely out of control!

The kind of love
that feels like Divinity creating
and loving through
you,
moment to moment.

Grace Comes in Many Forms

Imet Noa just hours after my mom called to tell me she was about to
commit suicide. I was twenty-nine, and it was a chilly November day
in New York City. I was saying goodbye to Anne and Joe, the two editors
I was working with on a documentary for Vice about the women and
customers in a New Mexico truck stop strip club, when my phone rang.
I answered and heard choked sobs on the line.

"Mom, what's going on?"

"I need to give you instructions on what to do with Sophie. I'm
going to kill myself tonight. I can't do it anymore."

Sophie was my mother's adorable geriatric pug that snored and
snorted like an old man.

"Mom, what? What the hell is going on? You cannot do this."

I began to yell into the phone, which is not how you are supposed
to talk to somebody who has just told you they are going to kill themselves, but it just came out. I was nowhere close to calm, rational, or
soothing. I was angry. Livid. The room swirled around me, and suddenly I was Dorothy in the middle of the tornado.

"Mom, you are not allowed to kill yourself. You are NOT! I'm calling
your therapist. Give me her number, now, please."

I called the therapist, who was surprisingly chill, nonchalant even.
My mother had been seeing her for about ten years, so with all the
gusto of someone who had clearly been here before, she said, "It's a
cry for help, she is okay," and some other bullshit. I wanted to throw
the phone at her head, but she was in Georgia and I was in New York.

I was in the throbbing, bloody heart of my Saturn Return, and it was all getting to be too much for me. It was a strange time on the path, a dive into something darker and deeper than my spiritual path had previously revealed, a time when I walked in shadows and had much to learn from them. First, there had been the ex-girlfriend who'd threatened to commit suicide when I broke up with her. Then there was my stint with a wealthy older lover who exhibited stalkerish behavior after I broke up with him. A few months prior, I had woken up to find my roommate's Australian friend on top of me in the dark, trying to have sex with me. And now my mom was threatening to kill herself? I was beginning to wonder what I'd done in a past life to deserve all of this.

My friend Kai was hosting a karaoke birthday party in Koreatown that night, and I was meeting my friend Adina for sushi on Astor Place before. Adina was a newer friend. We met dancing at a party in the East Village called Choice C*nts. She was getting her master's in gender politics and psychology at Columbia and was immersing herself in the queer scene for research. I called Adina and told her I had just talked my mom out of killing herself and that I needed a drink. Possibly a few. And a cigarette.

I didn't know what shock felt like in my body until I answered my mom's call that day. It was like I had been catapulted outside of my body and into deep survival mode. Years later, a Nigerian-American shaman in Hollywood told me that part of my soul fragmented that night, and in our session he yelled at the hidden part of my soul and said, "What, you think you can leave her? Get back here!" But in that moment, in the chilly office in the Tower Records building on West Fourth Street, something came online, and it said, "DO NOT fall apart." I had no one to catch me, so falling apart wasn't an option. I was an only child, and my closest friends were far away. There was no safe space, no circle of women, no spiritual community. I had given all that up when I moved back to New York.

By the time I got to Kai's karaoke party, I was already tipsy. After many calls to my uncle, my former stepdad, and my mom's therapist, my mom had decided to live and was on her way to check herself into a mental hospital.

So, why did I decide to still go to the party? I didn't know Kai very well, but the thought of getting on the train and going back to Williamsburg alone sounded awful. My roommate was in Tulum with her new girlfriend, and the apartment was empty. Karaoke and other humans sounded much safer.

Facing my mother's mental health struggles wasn't anything new; it had been part of my childhood, a childhood that now seemed to be spilling into adulthood. I had sought healing in my first ayahuasca ceremony and two peyote ceremonies the year before, where I had purged and cried and felt like I was ready to let go of the past. I had also been going to therapy off and on since I was twenty-one, so the concept of healing wasn't new to me, but it was taking longer than expected.

Before I returned to New York, I'd been devoted to my spiritual and artistic path, living close to my soul. I had spent time in Italy with yogic monastics, practicing meditation and celibacy and wearing communal clothes. I had felt alive and safe living in Portland at a community-focused home, where I recycled my bath water, wore only thrifted clothes, and did pagan rituals in the yard under the moon. I'd had space to breathe there, go slow, and be loved and held. Working at a juice bar and riding my vintage Schwinn home in the rain, I'd felt free. I'd fallen in love with an artist who lived in a storage unit overlooking the river. He took me on picnics in cemeteries and read me the romantics in my tub. He had a tattoo over his heart that said "land mine" in Cyrillic. He'd grown up in Kentucky, dumpster dived at McDonald's as a child while living out of a car with his mom and sister, and later became a fixture in the alt-art scene in Portland, where I met him playing his accordion at a show.

Now there I was in New York, still wrestling with my karma, my addictive behaviors, my spiritual practice, my art, and my childhood in a messy, albeit dedicated, way. Only now I had agents at the fancy-dancy Creative Artists Agency and was making films for Vice, being invited to fancy parties, and wearing jeans that were too tight. I had been invited into the queer Brooklyn hipster glitterati, my morning meditations were getting shorter, and my nights were getting later.

The bhakti-loving hippie artist who sang "Hare Krishna" and watered her plants with her moon blood was on hold for now.

That night, I arrived to the party leaning my head out of the taxi window, listening to the Chromatics, and steeping in the existential void of my own pain and aloneness. I was tipsy from dinner and had convinced the cab driver to let me smoke in the cab. Smoking was something I had picked up and put down hundreds of times, but for now I was IN IT. I submitted myself to this time, the nihilistic descent of Inanna's underworld, and like a crow sitting on a tombstone, smoking was a great accessory to those times.

I wish I could remember what I wore that night to Kai's birthday party, but I don't. I do remember when I first saw Noa. I was sitting across the room, and she grabbed the karaoke mic and began to sing "Stand by Your Man." She was wearing an oversized sweater and had an "I don't give a fuck" air about her that was magnetic. She was thin and blonde and had the feeling of a faraway place. I watched her as she sang offkey in a low, raspy voice with zero embarrassment or shame. There were no modest giggles at herself, just her full commitment to the song. When she put the mic down, I walked straight over to her. I don't think I thought about why or how I would start a conversation with her. That is what alcohol can do, I suppose: take away inhibitions and thus change the course of your life.

I asked in a deadpan tone, "Do you want to have coffee with me sometime, or do you just want to come home with me now?"

She looked at me and grabbed her coat.

I gave Kai a hug on the way out, and she said, "Ah, you met Noa! Fresh off the boat from Israel. Have fun."

I'd never loved a small, blonde, long-haired woman. The few women I had loved were butch, but Noa was an alien, not really masculine or feminine. She was just herself. Her bedroom was completely empty except for a long black whip on the wall, a pink jellyfish toy on the floor, and a steaming radiator. It could have been an installation in the Whitney Biennial.

Noa became my lifeline while I was in constant worry and fear as my mother was in the mental institution getting electroshock therapy, then in a halfway house trying to find her ground. As she lost her ground, I lost mine, too. Noa held me in her way, and with her thick Israeli accent, said, "Don't worry, Alexandra. Let's have another glass of wine and dance." She wasn't a meditator, she didn't sit in ceremonies, and she didn't pray, but her grandmother had been shot in the shoulder in the Holocaust when she was fifteen, had stuffed bread in her wound and sat in a hole in the ground in silence for a week until it was safe to come out, so somewhere in her bones Noa knew suffering and wasn't afraid of it. She could feel hurt. She grew up feeling the giant suffering and pain of a whole people, and that is a very deep spiritual practice. It expands the heart and soul in many ways. Because of that, she could hold me in my suffering without being afraid of what I was going through.

As long as we don't dare to feel what hurts, we cannot be with or hold others in their hurt. With our hearts closed, we cannot feel compassion for the pain of others. When we fear pain and suffering, we hold life at bay. But when we have stared suffering in the eye without turning away, as many cultures have been forced to do, there is a spiritual merit gained that cannot be bought or taught. It is a soul initiation into greater love, compassion, and openheartedness. This is not less spiritually powerful than meditating for ten days at a time. No, no, no. The lessons and practice come in different ways for different people. Being with pain is a practice. Staying in the room while others suffer is a practice. Being with and present in your own suffering is a practice.

Noa's spirituality was different from mine. It didn't look like seated meditation or chanting or prayer. It was simply an ability to be with suffering, to be unafraid of suffering, to love in the face of suffering. And because of this, she was the perfect companion in a time when I felt I was drowning in pain, and I am forever grateful for her.

We all have moments in life when we feel like we are drowning, when everything that could go wrong seems to. Those are the moments when we can ask for grace. And grace will come. **As trite as**

it may sound, when our worlds feel like they are falling apart, there is a tremendous opportunity to surrender control and stop resisting the lessons that are incoming. There is also an ongoing opportunity to ask for help, to pray for grace, to pray for mercy. Grace may come on a quiet day with gentle rain. Grace may come in the form of a human who makes you laugh and pours you a cup of tea (or sings karaoke with you!). Grace may be a movie that reminds you that this human experience has included a lot of suffering for a great many people, and you are not immune. Your suffering actually brings you closer to the whole of humanity, as does your joy, your desire for love, and your ability to love. We must release the notion that our suffering is unique. It is not. We all hurt. We can either let that separate us or draw us nearer to one another. Choose the latter. It is time.

Dare to Feel

REFLECTIONS

- What time in your life do you consider a "dark night of the soul" or a rock bottom moment for you? What feelings come up for you as you contemplate this period in your life?

- What emotions were present during this time, and how did you deal with them?

- What beliefs about yourself were present during this time, and where did they come from?

- How does that time compare to where you are now?

- What were the major spiritual lessons of this time? What did you learn about daring to feel, or not daring to feel, amidst these rocky waters of living?

- If you are in it right now, consider what lessons are arising. What feelings, what core wounds, and what remedies and practices are holding you now? What might come after you move through this portal of intensity? What newness is on the horizon for you? Is there a sliver of hope in the distance?

RITUAL FOR A DARK NIGHT OF THE SOUL

Set your ritual space. Sit and write out the story of your dark night of the soul. Make it into a myth, tale, or legend, humorous or dark, or turn it into lyrics for a blues or folk song. Talk about the strengths and weaknesses in your lead character, the trials and tribulations they faced, and how they finally found the pot of gold in the lessons they went through. When you're done, share it: record it in a voice memo, send it to a trusted friend and ask if they will witness you, read it to a favorite tree or to your altar or to a photo of you as a child—or simply let it live in the wind.

REALLY FREE

You think you're free,
and then you hang out with someone who is REALLY FREE!
Who loves BIG!
Dances BIG!
Laughs BIG!

And just being around them is better than any
ten-day Vipassana meditation retreat,
any "Find Your Purpose" workshop,
any trip to Burning Man!

When someone's presence is your medicine,
they are giving you a gift of awe,
of wonder,
of silly,
of being sung to,
of being fed cake,
of having your tears licked off your cheeks,
of dancing in a techno club where you feel higher than ever
off nothing but Love,
of laughing until you cry out, "Again, again!"

They are reminding you what it means to be really free.

Daring but Not Feeling

The sun peeped in and spilled onto my face like it always did on an LA morning. The California sun is fun for a bit, but it exposes you, shining on everything. In that much light, there is nowhere to hide. My head throbbed as I laid in bed. I couldn't remember how I got home, but my alarm gently dinged, waking me from my slumber. Thank God for smartphones. I had thirty minutes to get myself together for a pickup shoot for our TV pilot, but my body felt heavy as lead. Despite the all-too-familiar feeling of the consequences of a big night out, I managed to get out of my queen-sized bed, put some clothes on my naked body, and stumble to the bathroom to get some makeup on my puffy face. My hand shook as I attempted to draw on my winged black eyeliner as straight as possible, and a dark cloud of shame began to swallow me, like a monster who had been waiting to say, "You dirty little slut. You whore. You addict. See, I told you! What the hell are you doing with your life?" I looked into my eyes in the mirror and did not recognize myself. I just saw the drops of blood from the claws of shame that pierced my skin.

My artistic collaborator was coming over soon, and I couldn't let her see me like that. I had to pull it together. Ever since I cheated on my ex-girlfriend with my college sweetheart a few months back, my whole life had crumbled in front of me. I had been living a happy lesbian life in my apartment on the border of Williamsburg and Greenpoint. We had plants, we knew our local baristas, and we had been a part of a community of artists and queer folks that felt like home. Things were expanding in both of our film careers. I had just wrapped the second season of my comedy web show and was now filming the TV pilot for the documentary series I had co-created. But I was unhappy. Even with fabulous agents, even with invites to the cool-kid parties, I was dreadfully unhappy. I was living what looked to be an amazing, glamorous life, but my deeper self, my soul, my spiritual self, was buried and gasping for oxygen.

I had gotten up the courage to leave New York and head to Los Angeles for a sunnier, "slower" life. At least, that was what I told myself. But there I was, doing the same old bullshit. New city. Same me. Even though my career was rising, I was at an all-time low on the inside. I was still on my spiritual path in many ways but lacking in community, teachers, and mentors, instead looking to Hollywood ambition as my life's leader. And it wasn't working. Some of my friends seemed to be able to stay true to their spiritual path while also living life in Hollywood, so why wasn't it working for me?

My hungover mind flashed back to the night before, and shame coursed through my body as I attempted to put rose blush on my cheeks. This time the shame came like a heavy freeze. My breath caught in my chest, and everything stopped. I dropped the blush in the sink, where it shattered into three big chunks that I carefully placed back in their case with a sigh.

That dreadful, heavy shame came from my first time at a sex party the night prior. I was so overwhelmed by the sexual energy in the room that I drank a bucket of tequila to numb my sensitivity. In retrospect, I think alcohol at sex parties is dangerous. With everyone's inhibitions out the window, how can we distinguish a yes from a no?

I'd walked into a downtown LA loft the night before with my blonde bombshell friend, who was a well-known writer with a successful TV show. She and I made some jokes about whether the people there were going to be hot or not, and we also made a code for "I want to leave," which I had forgotten by my third tequila. We walked down the poorly lit hallway and through a big iron door. We were instructed to leave our clothes there, but I kept my panties on. Of course I planned for the occasion and wore a black lace set that had good enough coverage to make me feel like I was a sexy vixen at a daytime pool party. I was clear, though, that I would not have sex with anyone. I was there to feel it out. I was curious about all things, and though this kind of thing had gotten me into trouble in the past, I felt capable of being in a room with many sexed-up humans without losing my shit or getting it on with ten people.

We were accompanied by a producer from the TV network I was working with on my pilot, who my friend knew, which made the scenario feel a bit tricky. I was in a business relationship with the network, hoping they would greenlight my pilot TV show, and there I was stripping down to my undies with one of their key producers. My creative collaborator would NOT approve of this. I could almost feel her gaze upon me even though she wasn't there. She'd looked at me with disgust when I betrayed my ex-girlfriend and shattered my life overnight. I could feel her disapproval for this moment, too.

A tall, shirtless man with a greasy bun and a wide gap between his front teeth offered me a massage, to which I said, "No thanks, but I would love a drink." He fetched me a shot of Patrón, and I kept the bottle close. I was terrified to be sober amidst the smacking of skin, wet sounds, pumping bodies, and moans. Though I was not afraid of sex, I had not been close to so many penises in a while. I had been in exclusively lesbian relationships for some years, and the pumping penetration felt violent to my system. It felt new, strange, and too much for me to bear without alcohol.

Next thing I knew, I was cuddling with the producer. He was the only person in the room who felt safe. He was an NYC-turned-LA Jewish intellectual hipster with dark hair and a mildly toned body that didn't scream "I go to the gym daily!" He felt way safer for me than the Burning Man poly crowd with man buns, ripped abs, and coconut oil massages. Though he was the one person I should not have been cuddling with because he was essentially a work colleague, that was not the first time I had cozied up to someone I was potentially going into business with. It had happened in New York, and my creative collaborator was pissed at me when I dated the Oscar-winning lesbian producer who was a higher-up at a company we were dying to work with. But none of that seemed to matter at the sex party. I wanted to be nestled in someone's arms because the sounds of flesh pounding and smacking were making me dizzy. He and I were both shocked and giggling and almost using each other as a buffer to keep strangers from trying to have sex with us. And that's what we did. To our right was a well-known sex therapist with a buzzy TED Talk who had each orifice filled to the brim with Man Bun and two other meaty men. The sounds of her full throat gurgling and gagging and the smells of wet smacking flesh wafting my way were enough for me to reach for the Patrón again.

I had longed for places where sexuality was freely and openly expressed, but something felt wrong there. Something in my body screamed "No!" Was it my conditioning? Was I a prude under a cool badass sexy chick veneer? No, that wasn't it. It was still there, this split between my spirituality and sexuality. Just because it was a more open, loving environment didn't mean people there were treating sex as sacred. In fact, it felt like the opposite. It felt hedonistic to me. Like people gulping down so much sex because their grandmas and mamas didn't get to. But they were free now, so why not? That was my perception in the moment. It felt off in my body, too much, too scary, so I kept drinking in an attempt to numb all the feelings in my body. I was trying to be cool and fit in, but I betrayed myself. Inside of me, a little girl was crying, begging to feel safe, and I locked her away and drowned her out with each sip of tequila.

Eventually, in a drunken stupor, with my inhibitions and judgment away on an all-inclusive vacation paid for by Patrón, a couple convinced me to "play" with them. The rest was all a haze, and eventually someone helped me call an Uber. I didn't recall the ride home. I usually was not a blackout drinker, but something about the immensity and intensity of the sexual energy was too much for me. I couldn't be with it. So I drank it away.

And now I stood with shame in the sublet I perfunctorily moved into with four strangers on the east side of LA, all my belongings in a storage unit in Brooklyn. As I looked in the mirror, I saw a woman in pain, just like Sia sang in her hit song "Chandelier": "I'm just holding on for tonight . . . Party girls don't get hurt . . . here comes the shame, here comes the shame . . ." My eyeliner was jagged, I was shrouded by shame, and my heart was crying. *Where am I? Who am I?* I had gotten lost in the land of cool kids, famous kids, parties, LA scenes, and NY nights. I used to be a gal who did rituals under the moon, who sang to fairies, who wrote for the sake of writing, who rarely drank too much, who sang while she walked down the street and rode her bike, who had potlucks with friends and laughed and laughed. What had happened to me?

That night was the catalyst for some real changes. Waking up and not remembering how I had gotten home scared me. That wasn't the me I knew. Drinking that much was also not me. I realized I was running from feeling the truth that I couldn't do it anymore. I couldn't keep up the cool girl image. I couldn't schmooze and booze at the parties. I couldn't be on the phone with agents I was trying to please. I couldn't live within a dream for more, more, more. Longing for my "big break" was breaking me. I was already broke, exhausted, and lonely, and I was desperately trying to recover my spiritual truth, my values . . . me. Everything in me attempted to avoid a massive change of path that was determined to happen whether I liked it or not.

I slowly made my way out of Hollywood and began to find out how I could live as an artist on my spiritual path without betraying my integrity and truth. I stopped drinking completely for a while, until I was clear enough inside to trust that I wouldn't drink to escape. I went through grief and pain as I split from my creative collaborator. It felt like a divorce. I had no friends for a while. I went to sound baths and crystal shops alone in LA. I cried on long hikes. I became no one, and it felt incredibly lonely. Once I started feeling again and listening to my heart and the little girl within, so much grief arose. I had a list a mile long of moments when I had abandoned myself to look cool or keep it together. I started to pick through them, one by one, to mourn them, to cry over them, and to let them go. I spent what felt like years alone, crying, praying, and meditating. I returned to my spirituality and recommitted to a sacred way of living. I let go of the phase of melding self-betrayal with sexual exploration, and I approached sex with sobriety and honor. Slowly I began to forgive myself, the curious explorer, the wild woman, the lonely little girl—all of me got called home. I was finding my heart again. I was listening to the little girl inside of me and cradling her close. I was starting to feel, and I was starting to heal.

Have you ever looked in the mirror and been unable to recognize the face looking back at you? Have you ever felt the bruising mix of shame and regret eat you bit by bit? We have all had moments when we betrayed our knowing. When we strayed from our truth. This is part of being human. We couldn't know our center if we didn't veer from it once in a while. The important piece is that we come back. We create touchstones in our lives that lead us home. We leave clues in a dark forest, and we follow the trail back to our selves. Sometimes this looks like trusted friends who call us out. Sometimes a guide. Sometimes family. Sometimes it is simply our own intuition that is nudging us back to the truth of who we are.

These moments in life are important. They create lasting imprints, so we do not have to redo them. Once we know what it feels like to abandon our truth, we can say, "I don't want to do that again." We have a deep, full-body knowing of what that feels like, and in moments when we start to self-abandon, we can notice quickly and come back home. This requires tenderness, compassion, and forgiveness. We can access those qualities always. They are within us, always accessible.

Part of being on this path is diving into hidden shadows, exploring them, and pouring love into them. There we see what we are really longing for: underneath surface cravings for sex or fame or money, we feel the deep longing to know ourselves as love. We feel the longing to belong, or the longing to be free.

Dare *to* Feel

REFLECTIONS

- What judgments do you hold about any past actions that carry the flavor of regret? What are you still holding onto? What have you forgiven?

- What does it feel like in your body and your psyche when you abandon your knowing or ignore your intuition?

- What does it feel like to come home to your truth?

- What moments can you recall where you ignored your truth? If you had dared to feel, how might things have played out differently?

RITUAL FOR SELF-FORGIVENESS

Light some candles, turn off your phone, and set up a mirror in a space where you won't be interrupted. This is best done at night or at dawn, but it can be done any time you feel called. Find a comfortable position, and call to mind any times when you abandoned yourself because it felt too scary or inconvenient to dare to feel. Now look into your own eyes and say, "I'm sorry."

Then set a timer for five minutes and go deeper with your self-forgiveness by gazing into your own eyes and speaking to yourself in more depth now, allowing a conversation to emerge. Practice compassion for the version of you who shied away from feeling by saying things like, "I know you were doing your best. I forgive you. I see you. I am here." Or "It was a really confusing time; you didn't have the support you needed; I will be here for you next time." Find your own voice there. Stay with it even when it feels uncomfortable. Feel for a shift in your relationship with the part of you that is asking for forgiveness.

ODE TO THE WILD MAIDEN

Were you once very wild?
Did you do things you wouldn't be able
to speak of at most dinner parties?
That would make your grandma roll over in her grave?
Do you carry fleshy secrets you wonder if you'll ever utter again?

Did you too try many wild things?

Were you curious, playful, adventurous, and free
on behalf of your own becoming a woman
and really knowing yourself?

And your flesh
and your edges?

Have you lived fully in pursuit of this knowing?

Bouncing between "good girl" phases
and then to the opposite extremes of wildness and play?

Do you also not regret tasting the delights of being human deeply?

Drinking of life fully?
Playing richly?
Late nights?
And saying yes
instead of no?

Do you carry regret and shame for your adventures,
or wear the scars proudly with laughter and a smile?

Sure, sometimes the youthful risks of the budding wild woman
resulted in heartache and pain,
but wasn't there also liberation from societal constructs?

Around the body,
around sex,
and around loving?

All the wild soul-making memories sit
in the treasure chest of YOU!

Maybe some will go with you to the grave,
others you will whisper over tea
and sunsets
or to a therapist
or to God!

Dissolving the shame of tasting life fully,
of being a woman who loves big
and who has a strong resting bitch face
and a hearty laugh,
her inner good girl mostly laid to rest.

Isn't it these moments
that have made the heart we have now?
And if so,
shall we say thank you?

To the wild nights of passion
and even the morning headaches,
the tears, and the fights . . .

Thank you to all the love
that has loved each and every one of us!

Man,
woman,
butch femme,
every position,
every kiss!

What fun were those hungry days,
looking for Soul Love in every eye,
on every train,
in every bar,
wondering,
Is it you?

God,
Goddess,
Divine
One
?
Is
it
YOU?

Risking Our Messy Feelings
to Be Seen

We were sitting in Sah's East Village apartment, half-eaten samosas on the table, looking at a map of India and planning our upcoming pilgrimage, when Moun looked at me and smiled and said, "You know, there won't be a Dry Bar on every corner!" My heart dropped down like an elevator, landing with a plink into the basement of my being. Ouch.

Okay, time out. Let me explain what Dry Bar is to those of you who perhaps think it's a place to get an alcohol-free martini. It's actually a chain of hair blow-dry spots, where you pay someone to wash and style your hair in under an hour. For context, I must say, I have wild, curly hair that I have worn curly the better part of my life, save for the hair straightening accident where my mom's friend gave me a perm in a basement when I was eleven, and a swath of my hair fell out. At age thirty-three, I had started blow-drying my hair out. It felt fun to do something different, and it made me feel more professional, like a movie star on social media, glossy and glam.

That aside, I was in shock, staring at Moun while she looked at me kindly, the samosas sitting beside the map of India, my blood beginning to boil. Did Moun think I was so attached to my blowouts that I would have trouble in India? That having wild hair would prevent me from enjoying a spiritual pilgrimage?

My heart sped up as I began to feel triggered and said, "What? What is that supposed to mean?"

"I just want to make sure you know India is not like here," she replied gently.

I paused in that moment, my heart breaking just a little. I thought, *Shit, does she not know me?* She knew one version of me, with a blowout, eyelash extensions, a book deal, and an Instagram following. It hadn't occurred to me that she didn't know the woman who had worked her ass off since she was twelve, who nannied for rich people and cooked in their kitchens, who slept under the stars at the Rainbow Gathering, who got clothes from free piles and thrift stores, who traveled around Brazil in a bus with a backpack, who took the Greyhound alone, who had just paid off her student loan debt and not long ago had given up her EBT card and Medicaid. My heart hurt in that moment; one innocuous joke from her had touched a deep wound in me of feeling unseen and judged, feeling one-dimensional. It was almost like one of my great fears had come true: I felt I was being judged on my appearance, by my work and stature, and not by my insides. That was new for me.

I managed to shrug it off that night, or at least I tried to. I defended myself by saying I had traveled around the world alone and had been to plenty of remote places. I would be fine. But inside, I wondered, *How many times in life do we meet someone in one way and not really know or ask who they are beyond that?* I also wondered, *Are my blowouts making me look like someone I am not?!*

Hair is complex, and the story of one person's hair is often a big deal for them, a cultural signifier, a marker of stature, money, subculture, and broader ethnicity. A lot of us have tenderness and insecurity around our hair, and we often can't hide it. It's much like skin. It's just there. We can adjust it, but it says on the outside who we are. It never doesn't make a statement. I was definitely the only white girl with hair that was textured beyond slick and straight in my elementary school; in high school there was one other person with big hair, who was half Jewish, and she was the only Jewish person I knew until I moved to New York. I was determined to keep my hair curly once I learned how to care for it from the women at the salon where I worked as a fifteen-year-old. They would say, "Let it be curly! It's beautiful." But I would try and brush it out and pull it back, and it looked a frizzy mess. Until one day one of the women showed me how to use hair gel and mousse; teenage me felt liberated! Since then, I'd been devoted to my curls, but at thirty-three years old, I wanted a change. My former life had crumbled, and my new look was symbolic of me starting anew. I had left my hipster Brooklyn queer filmmaker vibes to pivot into the wellness world, and I needed something to mark it externally.

This was why Moun's comment struck deep into my core identity of not wanting to appear like someone who cared about blowouts more than spiritual pilgrimages. Had my choice to blow out my hair betrayed the true me, and now people only knew me as this? I wanted to make a post on Instagram saying, "I have never been included in the pretty straight hair girl club. And now I am, and it feels terrible. I'm sorry."

The morning after the India planning meeting, I called Moun and said tenderly, "I am scared you don't really know me." She tried to tell me multiple times that she had just been joking. It was like one of those "What Happens When Leo Teases Pisces" memes, and the Pisces is in a tunnel of emotion and reflection for a week while the Leo has moved on in ten seconds flat, ready to dance and play. I was that Pisces. I was looking for the deeper meaning in the question of why I was so triggered by that comment. Moun promised me that she didn't think I was superficial, and that she was really just teasing, which was an actual love language in her family. She reassured me that she did know me. She knew I had lived unconventionally and had had lots of adventures. She knew I had made weird ritual art films and sat in a sweat lodge and lived in an ashram and worked at a truck stop strip club for my documentary, where I had slept in a dilapidated motel and shot machine guns in the desert.

Why was I so protective of my inner rebel and unconventional side? I had earned it from hitchhiking and sleeping in weird places and making experimental art. But where was she now? Was she so hidden under the lashes and blowout that it didn't matter anyway? That question stayed with me, and in her ability to call it forth in me, I came to see Moun as a friend who was actually a deep spiritual teacher. She could touch deep places in me, and I in her, and there was so much that came forward between us. I trusted her to call me forward. I trusted her to show me my tender spots, where I was holding back, where I was afraid.

By our third week of traveling through India and Nepal, I was exhausted. I was filled with so much goodness, so much newness, and I felt stretched in a delicious yet slightly painful way. We had traipsed through magical places, praying, laughing, crying, and singing; it was the trip of a lifetime.

One day, we spent the day at a monastery in Kathmandu receiving a tantric Buddhist initiation, and after, Moun and I and the rest of our friends pattered down the hill to the entrance of the monastery to look for cabs. Night had fallen over Kathmandu, and from atop the hill, we could see the twinkling lights below. Even through a layer of smog, the city looked magical. There were no cabs waiting outside the monastery; it was not the arrivals terminal at JFK. Nope. Not here. I imagined all the cab drivers at home, eating dinner with their families, laughing and talking loudly. We went to the monastery office to try and call one anyway, but we soon found that we weren't the only ones to have that brilliant idea; the office was crowded and noisy with French, German, Spanish, and English intermingling in the night air.

Perhaps the noise and uncertainty about how we would get home stressed me out a bit. It was a long walk down to the city in the dark, so I tried my best to help Moun find our way on a map, but the truth is, I am horrible with maps and directions. Before Google Maps, I would print out MapQuest directions for everywhere I went. Google Maps was liberation for me! I stood across from Moun and fired off problem-solving questions in her direction.

"Love, how will we get down the hill? Is there a taxi service? Maybe we can borrow the phone and call?" I pushed in on her with increasing anxiety.

Finally, she looked at me and said, "You're type A. Why don't you figure it out?"

I don't remember the *exact* thing I said or did that pushed her to the edge. I imagine I was being extra anxious and pushy, and I imagine her response was justified.

India and Nepal had been doing their deep healing magic on us from the day we arrived. In that tiny room at the mouth of the monastery in Nepal, I felt the power of Shakti, Kali, Divine Mother, and the turning of the wheel of karma in each interaction between everyone in the group. I felt a mystical shadow worker, a stirrer of deep pains and hidden wounds, coming forward in my time there.

I snapped back like I had never heard of spiritual practice. "What did you say to me?" I practically yelled across the room, a hand perched on my hip as if I was a reality TV star. "How dare you!"

Isn't it wild how you can sit at the feet of one of the most famous Buddhist teachers in the world and get a spiritual initiation that is meant to speed up your karma, and twenty minutes later you have forgotten everything you learned?! Or perhaps that is exactly what is meant to happen. Perhaps that kind of initiation heats things up so they're ready to burst free from your insides like mini volcanos erupting karmic ooze you have the opportunity to wash clean as it is exposed.

I think that's what happened that night. I got a chance to examine my reactivity, my oversensitivity, my aversion to teasing, my tendency to be overbearing and anxious in the face of uncertainty. I got to sit with it.

As I walked down the hill to our friends up ahead, trailing Moun by eight feet or so, a lightning bolt of clarity hit me on my head.

"This is ridiculous!" I shouted. "We are walking down a hill in a magical foreign country after a highly spiritual day in a huff, mad at each other. This is not okay. I will not do this!"

The path down the hill was pitch black. There were no streetlamps or even a sidewalk. I yelled again, "Moun!" Running a little to catch up with her, I continued, "We are too smart for this. We can choose to do something different right now." I wasn't trying to be a saint, putting my ego aside to rush in and save the day. No, no, no. That was also my discomfort—I hated sitting in the rupture, so I needed to attempt to make a repair.

Moun took the "Let's give it a moment to breathe" route. Fair enough. But boy, oh boy, that didn't work for me! The more space she took as she moved ahead, the more determined I became. I wanted to solve the problem and repair it quickly, but she wanted space to breathe. She walked ahead in the dark, her tall silhouette making shadows on the cobblestones. I pulled my shawl around my body and tried to be patient, but I was not having any of it. I was determined to fix it.

I caught up to her on the road, and we walked side by side as tears fell onto our matching red shawls.

"Why do you take things so personally?" she wondered out loud.

"Because I am a sensitive, empathic, only child, a daughter of people who didn't recover from their traumas, and I just feel everything now. Before I didn't feel nearly as much, but now I feel it all." I responded. "I'm learning to not take things as personally, and to feel in moderation, but I need time."

She tried to understand me, and I did the same for her. I had never been teased as an act of love. Except by my dad. And perhaps it was a wound that needed to rise. When it did in that monastery, it was perfect. It was exactly what I needed to feel.

That night on that hill under the stars, we cried. We laughed. And then we fought some more. In this dance, we released whatever trigger was coming up for both of us the best we could.

The conversation continued over the next twenty-four hours. In the morning we sat on one of the tiny twin beds in our shared room and talked. Things came up from the months before, things we didn't address in the moment. Moun revealed things I had done and ways I had been unconscious that broke my heart. I held her hands in mine and apologized.

"I wish you would have told me how that hurt you," I said. We were both learning, and we were both humbled by the love and the parts of ourselves we must face to show up to our friendship. I got us lattés, and we eventually sat by the window in the guest house café, where there was a little bit of Wi-Fi. Our shoulders touched as we sat in silence, writing on our phones and blasting our hearts to thousands of followers online. Because that was what we did at that time. Our hearts were free and open to all. We shared a croissant, and the moment was tender and true. We were closer now. There was more trust in place.

I am grateful for that rupture, and all the ruptures that reveal truth. It was actually perfectly timed. I thank the tantric initiation that had not allowed us to ignore anything or hold the burden of unmet needs and painful moments, but instead allowed them all to come up to be washed and cleansed in the holy fires.

The experience brought us so much closer. I was able to eat my slice of humble pie and claim the type-A part of me, the little girl who had learned that if I take care of things, plan them, and control them, then I can stay safe. The one who didn't want to sit in conflict and couldn't bear being mad at her best friend, and who also needed to learn how to not take everything so personally and let people have some space.

Because I dared to feel, I was available for that lesson, and I remain highly grateful for it. It's not every day that friends you trust are honest with you, and you don't say, "Fuck you!" and move on. It takes courage for a friend to be that real with you. They are taking a risk because, like me, you may freak out. And no one wants to deal with a diva having a meltdown, especially on a dark street in Nepal. But a real friend will risk it. And sometimes it's messy when things come up. It's not all PC and perfectly communicated. Sometimes it has to get a little heated for real intimacy to be born.

I knew Moun cared about our friendship because she was willing to get in the trenches with me, roll up her sleeves, examine some shit, get real without running when things got tough, and laugh over lattés after. She was willing to hold my hand as we walked together into the karmic clearing and healing we had come for.

Not all friendships can hold the openhearted path of deep feeling. Not all are available for that level of openness, heart workout, honesty, and healing. And that is okay. It takes a lot of trust and stable ground to do the deep work with a friend. Some friendships collapse when put to the test, some are fragile, some are casual, and some aren't strong enough to hold the transformation of the heart. But the ones that can face the grit of real intimacy are the ones that begin to feel like family. And those are the ones you can count on, come hell or high water, as they say in Georgia where I grew up. We all need a few friends like that. Friends who have our back and aren't scared of having tough conversations. Friends who also have their own relationship to growth and healing and know that's why we are in it together.

Dare
to
Feel

REFLECTIONS

- Which friends are you able to get into the trenches with and go super deep? What is it about these people that helps you dare to feel?

- Have you experienced any ruptures and disagreements as a result of being raw and honest with each other? Have you been able to repair them? If so, how?

- What created the safety for you to be honest in those friendships, and how can you consciously bring more of this to the other relationships in your life?

- Have you tried to go deep with a friend and share your heart and been rejected? How did this feel, and how did you respond?

RITUAL FOR GRATITUDE FOR A FRIENDSHIP

Set your ritual space. Write a letter of gratitude to a friend who has walked the transformational path of the heart with you. Share with them all the small moments that you recognize as having helped create the intimacy that could hold such a deep bond. If it feels right, send them the letter or read it to them in person if you dare; if you'd prefer to keep it private, tuck it away somewhere special and reference it when you need to remember that you are not alone on the path.

IF WOMEN WERE HONEST

Why do women lie to each other?

"You look AMAZING!"

"Thank you! You too! OMG! I am obsessed with you!"

Why do women exaggerate false niceties?

Like approval junkies,
sniffing at the powder of Fake.

What relief might come with saying,
"You know, you may feel me as cold. It's because I am jealous of you.
Thanks for bearing with me as I work through my own fears."

What illusion might be shattered with,
"That hardness you feel from me, well, I struggle with feeling like I'm
enough when I see how much you or others around me have achieved.
And it is mine to work with. You needn't change a thing."

What peace might come with,
"I know my hair looks great. Thank you. But I wear it this way to hide
what a mess I am on the inside today."

Perhaps this might open a door to the Realms of the Heart, and she might say,
"Oh, honey. I feel that way often too. Come here. Your truth is like a
breath of fresh air."

Or she may look at you funny, flash a fake smile, and turn back to her
phone.

Regardless, it's worth the risk.

Isn't it?

14

Daring to Be Honest

Before I entered the mundane garage turned dark and mystical temple, I slid my open-toed clogs off by the door, my apple red toenail polish reflecting light from the sky. I took a deep breath, excited and nervous to enter the room. I was always available for tough conversations, but I had a feeling this one was going to be extra hard. I was not on my turf. I was in the student position, a position traditionally of lesser power, and love clouded my clarity at times, as it could do for some teacher-student relationships. I had been walking with a commitment to my heart and its honesty and feeling for a few years now, and I felt I had the tools to meet whatever was coming as a part of my own transformation and healing.

I took a deep breath and opened the door, leaving the bright Santa Monica sun behind me. Two thick, red taper candles were lit on either side of a big mirror in the center of the room. In front of the mirror was a large book on a stand. I can't recall what the book was, but in my memory, it was some kind of mystical book, like a book of shadows.

My two teachers sat with perfect yogic posture on the floor on two meditation cushions, woman on left, man on right, corresponding with the body's energies of the feminine and masculine. They weren't too much older than me, and they were beautiful, radiant, and strong humans. Across from them was a third cushion placed in the center opposite them, which I quietly sat on. We were all there to attempt to find peace, to mediate a problem, and yet the air felt so dense, dark, and heavy. I could not feel my own heart in the space. No, not at all.

We all took deep breaths together before a masculine voice spoke: "I am going to lead us in a little meditation to ground into this moment. Let's all close our eyes."

I took a deep breath, relieved to be held by the darkness behind my eyes.

I had been their student for a year and a half at that point, and with them, I felt I had found some sort of spiritual community and home. I had done work-study with them, assisting them with their classes and events in exchange for free participation. In my eyes, I had given my best to each event I assisted, unconsciously attempting to be the perfect student, to "get it right" and gain their approval, whether I knew it or not. When I met them, I had just left my "old life" in New York and was in a period of deep healing and commitment to my spiritual path after a tough time.

Rebuilding my sense of self after my descent into my own personal underworld, I popped out on the other side into sunny Santa Monica, where I was bathed in green juice and sound baths and surrounded by happy, sunny people. It was the opposite of the New York artist intellectual hipster set I had existed within. I was open and hungry for belonging when I landed in Los Angeles, and something about that community felt like home. So, when my teachers asked if I would commit to working with them as their assistant for the coming year even though I was running my own business, writing my first book, and still directing TV commercials here and there, I said yes. I was flattered and excited by them wanting ME for the job. I felt I belonged. I felt special.

They were loving to me. They invited me in with open arms. They trusted me. I imagine it was vulnerable for them, too, to claim their need and see their business was growing and required support. They knew I was a hard worker. I had always kept my word and always showed up on time, excited to learn from them. We had developed a closeness. They trusted me, and that felt so good. I wanted to be in the community as a leader and keep learning from them.

Now that we were making it "official," they told me they wanted me to be in the program for the coming year as a paying client and also as an assistant for the year. I was confused. By the time the conversation came up, I had been doing work-study with them for the past twelve months, trading my time for their teachings and assisting them in exchange for experiencing their workshops. I was already assisting in many ways.

"We would like to have you in the program next year. It's a yearlong group, and it is going to go super deep."

Robert spoke to me over the phone as I stood outside the mall in Miami Beach, waiting for my father's then-wife to finish her post-Christmas shopping. I looked around at the bleakness of mall culture. Bags and bags of things, people lining up in hoards outside of The Cheesecake Factory, my father's wife with her silicone DD breasts. I was grateful I had found my way out of the places I had grown up in, that I had been taught that there is another way to live, that you get to choose what kind of life you want to live and what you want to prioritize. A stroller with two snot-nosed kids and a yelling mom pushed by me. Cars honked their horns, fighting for parking spots. I took a deep breath.

"Are you in?" they asked.

In that moment, I didn't realize the financial ins and outs of my commitment. I just knew I had found a new spiritual community, and they felt like home. As I walked back into the mall, I didn't quite think about the fact that I would be paying to be in the program and *also* assisting for free. It didn't make sense to me at the time, but I said yes because I was blinded by my desire to belong. Paying to be a part of the family didn't matter at first. I just wanted to be there.

But my real family and friends were all aghast when I told them that I had been asked to pay to be an assistant. I felt silly. I tried to justify to my friends that it was a special deal, that it would make sense in the long run. But slowly the fog of my desire for love and belonging cleared, and something just felt off. I looked at my budding business, my career that I was slowly building, the healing I was doing around my finances, and I realized it just wasn't right for me, and that my devotion and love for them were keeping me from getting real about my own truth.

At first I was terrified to tell them the truth. I was ashamed to say, "It doesn't feel right for me to pay you to keep working for you. I can either pay to be in your program as a student, or I can assist you. But it feels weird to me to do both." Being that honest scared the shit out of me. I didn't want to upset them. I didn't want to question their authority or integrity. So I lied. I lied. I lied to the people I loved. I lied to the people who had felt like family. It was shitty and cowardly. But I did it. I said I was just too busy with my work to take on the assistant job and that it didn't work with my schedule, and I was so sorry. I wrote a long email with all kinds of excuses because I was so terrified of upsetting "Mommy and Daddy" and losing their love, approval, and belonging.

Which was exactly what happened.

Back in the darkened room, we did a grounding meditation. I breathed deeply, knowing that I must speak my truth about why I backed out on my word. I had to own up to my lie, my people-pleasing, my craving for family and love, my wound of belonging. If only I could smooth it all over, pretend it was not a biggie, and shush it, but I couldn't. That one financial decision to trade money for love and commitment was symbolic, and something in me said no, and now I had to explain why, even though I felt like I wanted to vomit. How dare you tell the truth and explain in laymen's terms to your spiritual teachers that something doesn't feel right to you? I felt like I was being an arrogant tattle tale.

We all opened our eyes, and they stated the intention for the gathering: "To clear the energy between us about what happened." The light was very low except for flames from the red candles. I stayed silent, just breathing.

They spoke to me one at a time, but it all blended together.

"We trusted you. We trusted you to come through."

Tears began to fill my eyes. The idea that their love for me would end if I didn't say yes to the offer was beginning to hit me, and my heart broke.

"I lied," I said. "I'm so sorry. I wasn't honest that it just didn't feel right for me, and instead I made up an excuse about why I couldn't do it. I'm so sorry. But it just didn't feel right to me, and I was afraid to say that to you."

"Yes, the lie hurt us. Your honesty would have been a gift. We want you with us."

I sighed. I could feel myself wanting to do anything they asked, wanting to please them, wanting to not get thrown out of their hearts forever. Something in me could not abandon my own truth or integrity.

"We really thought you were a true practitioner. We were mistaken."

An invisible dagger struck me in the heart. I had broken their trust by not being honest, and they were gone.

We agreed to take some space to breathe into the situation and let it sit for a minute, but I felt I had spoken up against Mommy and Daddy and had been kicked out of their house. I was no longer part of the family. Once again, I was alone, and yet I was also set free.

I grieved this loss for a very long time. I was upset that I had lied to them, that I hadn't had the courage to be honest and say, "I have some ideas about the exchange. Can we talk about it?" My judgment clouded my love for them and made me unable to see that perhaps they, too, were fallible humans doing the best they could. They, too, had an unconscious, and their unconscious was bumping on mine like two dark clouds hovering around us, gifting us with an opportunity to bring something to light, into consciousness.

For me, it brought into the light my craving for belonging, my people-pleasing, my fear of speaking up, my quickness to lie to avoid telling the truth. I lost people I deeply loved, people who felt like family, and it was no easy loss. Losing spiritual community never is. It's like you finally left the family sitting at The Cheesecake Factory, staring at the blinking TVs, and you found the family that sits together and honors this life and the great mystery, the family that feels like a home you never had. But when its humanity is revealed, too, you run, terrified, or you realize that every family has its issues. No one is immune. **You realize the difference is that some families are open to healing those issues, and some are not. Some are meant to be forever family, and some are just lessons. The discernment is the painful part.**

You learn to let go of the ones that are stops on the journey, even though you wish they were forever homes. Then you hold tight the motley crew of spiritual friendships you do have because you know they are so valuable. They are everything. You've tasted life without them, and it hurts. You need them. You pour your love into them and fall to your knees in gratitude that they exist. **This is the healing: the family you create that sticks, that stays, that holds you and forgives you, even when you mess up.**

Dare
to
Feel

REFLECTIONS

- Have there been times when you were confronted with the humanity of your sacred spaces or spiritual leaders, whether it was a spiritual community or a religious organization?

- Have there been times when you have put someone on a pedestal only to discover that they have human failings, too?

- What did it feel like to have the illusion of spiritual leaders being perfect or not having their own shadows shattered?

- What were you hoping to gain from being part of the group, and what did you end up gaining as a result of feeling hurt or confused or outside of the group?

- Were any of your own shadows or blind spots revealed in the process? What did you learn about yourself as a result?

- Have you looked for a surrogate family at any point in your life? What feelings let you know when you have found a sense of kinship?

RITUAL FOR PAYING HOMAGE
TO THE HEART'S HUNGERS

Create a living homage to the hungers of your heart: what your heart longs for, is hungry for, yearns for . . . If you aren't sure, feel into what you want most in life. Let that be your heart's hunger. Create an art piece. An altar piece. First, find a symbol for the hungers of your heart: for love, belonging, family, home, whatever it is. This is your centerpiece. This could be a poem printed out. It could be an image of you at a particular time in your life. It could be a bundle of flowers and greenery. It could be a wedding ring. It could be a baby shoe. It could be an image of divine lovers. Gather any other objects around the symbol of your heart's hunger. If you have clay, mold it. If you have collage materials, create a collage. If you have fresh roses and want to use those on an altar or bedside, do so. Keep this homage to your heart's hunger close to you in your bedroom for one full lunar cycle, and as you pass it daily, send it prayers of compassion and love.

MAGIC SCHOOL

There is a direct path to learning the sacred arts of
internal alchemy
and transformation.

The path of lived experience,
which leads to wisdom.

Of course,
there is also
the path of knowledge and study.

But all of my initiations
in this life
have come from taking the direct path.

The path that requires a fighter's spirit and some fucking grit.

The path of blood, sweat, tears, failure, attempts, risks, and trials.

It ain't pretty, but it is magical.

Are you going to stay clean, studying magic inside all day?

Or will you come get dirty with me in life's arena?

15

The Heart's Hungers
That Blind

I've always had a pretty good intuition when it comes to people. However, at times I have overridden this intuition and convinced myself that so-and-so is "not thaaaaat bad" or "maybe I should just get to know them." Oftentimes, in my youth, my heart's hunger overrode my intuition. Also, seductive qualities clouded my ability to listen to my intuition, namely good looks and fame, to be humiliatingly frank. Not all the time, of course, but enough times that I have a few scars to speak for it. Sometimes the things that made me override my intuition were giving someone the "benefit of the doubt." There is a kindness in seeing the good in people first, but there is also a danger in *only* seeing the good in people.

I always say that when someone says, "Well, maybe," in a high-pitched voice, they are leaving their truth. You probably hear people do it all the time. Namely women. It has become pretty obvious to me that when our voices get high, we are no longer ourselves. We are in some sort of weird, fake, survival response. And this is how we get hurt—by leaving our centers and becoming people pleasey, or avoiding the unpleasant truths of the moment. It's not that we should only try to avoid hurt along the openhearted path, but we want to honor our knowing, our truth, our center, and not hurt ourselves. The transformational path of the heart means noticing the heart's blind spots and the feelings that arise to indicate which way to turn, what is truly happening, and create the wisdom of discernment within us.

One of the aforementioned scars came from an Adonis-like man in Los Angeles who I somehow found on social media. Though he was called Hunter, I think I was the one who hunted him first. Nevertheless, I was curious. At the time, I was exploring who I wanted to be with, and I was curious about "spiritual men in LA." That sentence gives me shivers where I sit now, but back then I was searching for love, and I was curious about these "conscious" men. I imagined men who had healed from childhood traumas, faced their internal misogyny, and saw their attachment patterns and issues and had perhaps worked on them in therapy, could take responsibility for their actions, and had a spiritual path, a relationship with God/Goddess/Divine and the mystery of Life! But that is a tall order. What I found in LA was more of a superficial "conscious man" who would stare deeply into your eyes as he introduced himself to you at a sound bath, a yoga studio, or the luxury grocery store Erewhon Market, where $17 smoothies are aplenty. Sometimes they would take a hearty, deep breath as they looked at you, staring deeply into you, because they had gone to a few men's work circles and learned that this is what "conscious men" do. Others did not get that behavioral memo and were squirrely and fidgety, on their phones and obsessed with social media and their abs, and didn't even pretend to be more evolved and enlightened. At least with those guys you didn't have to wonder much about who they were because the surface told quite a bit.

When I eventually met Hunter, he turned out to be the latter. Because he seemed so ab-obsessed (I judge) and I had never dated a person like that before, I kind of thought he was a hoot. Yes, a hoot. Like funny and ironic. I had always been with intellectual, artistic folks who could talk about French philosophers and early twentieth-century classical music, so the LA conscious ab guy was a new thing for me. The fact that he ran in a spiritual crowd (or so I thought) was a bonus; I had no idea what that even meant for him, but I was curious. He was tall, at least six-foot-three, with chiseled, dark, ethnically ambiguous features, 70K Instagram followers, and a few pictures of himself posing with well-known wellness leaders.

After I liked two of his Instagram pictures, he asked me out via a DM. He said he wanted to take me out to dinner and would drive to the east side of LA, where I lived at the time, to pick me up. Now, I thought that was real gentlemanly! How kind! He wanted to take me to Café Gratitude, a Venice Beach conscious-crowd haunt. I was game for the adventure to the west side, and because I ignored my intuition about this human, I easily convinced myself that it was okay to get into a car with a stranger because his Instagram showed him to be a "spiritual guy" with tons of followers and endorsements from some legit folks.

After he picked me up from Silver Lake in his gold Dodge Caravan, we began the drive westward. On the way to the restaurant, he said, "I forgot my wallet at home. I'll just swing by; it'll just take a second." I could see through it all, every minute of it. I chuckled to myself on the inside, but I was also too cavalier. At the time I was in it for the story, something I could tell my friends over dinner for a big laugh, instead of feeling into the deeper care for myself that I deserved. I thought he was harmless and kind of dumb, and I pretended I didn't notice his seduction plan. So when we pulled up to his apartment building and he asked if I wanted to come up for a second, I said, "Sure." The garage was seedy and dark, and staying in the car actually felt worse.

I knew I was walking into a trap. This is the problem with saying yes out of curiosity, or being "polite," or people pleasing, or leaning into your naiveté when you really know you should say no. It's like when you're a teenager who has been told that drugs and drinking and driving are bad, but you still do it because you're young, dumb, and curious, and/or perhaps have trouble saying no, which you will work on later in therapy. But in this scenario, I had already worked on boundaries in therapy, and I was not young and naïve. I was thirty-three years old. But my heart was hungry for love, and my soul was hungry for adventure and a good story, so I kept saying yes.

We walked into the building and down the hallway as several exposed bulbs blinked overhead like a B-movie horror film. Once we were inside, he finally revealed that it wasn't his apartment but his friend's, who was out of town, and that he usually lived in his van. My heart started to speed up a bit, and I simultaneously wanted to have a giant laugh and run. (Yes, multiple reactions can happen at once in a body-mind.) Now, I had nothing against a nomadic lifestyle, but I had recently dated two other California van-living guys and had decided that, given my desire for partnership and family, they were probably not the best choice. And it was becoming very clear that Hunter was not the best choice, either, in myriad ways.

He opened the apartment door as I kept telling myself he was harmless. The apartment had a mattress on the floor with two case-less pillows and a crooked, cheap Monet poster on the wall. As a writer, I took in the scene and kept reminding myself that this was going to make a great story. Meanwhile, Hunter talked nonstop about his super-food business, using all the spiritual buzzwords he had in his toolkit.

Now, here was where things got sticky. I knew Hunter was using spiritual lingo to seduce me, but I didn't know if he was innocent and horny or if he was a darker, more dangerous character. Because of his spiritual lingo, I chose to hope that he was just a little snaky but harm-less. He decided he wanted to give me Amazonian tobacco snuff that was blown up the nose. And he pulled out several bags of drugs and placed them on the floor. Mushrooms, MDMA, LSD.

Cute! I told myself. *He is playing show and tell!* It wasn't the first time some LA guy showed up to a first date with drugs. A year prior I went out with a famous actor who parked his car under the Hollywood sign and whipped out bags of molly *and* his penis on the way to our Soho House date. This wasn't my first rodeo, and I knew how to say no. I quickly got it that Hunter was not someone to trust, and I started to put my guard up. He poured us some reverse-osmosis water and added some drops to it, and at that moment, I asked to go to the restroom. It was a bad time to go, but I needed to. The bathroom had more dollar store art on the walls, and the toilet had a thick brown ring about the bowl.

This is me dating at thirty-three in LA. Wow, I thought with a heavy sigh as I stared into the stained toilet. Perhaps I was getting too old for this type of research. I wondered if I should hop into an Uber or if we were actually going to go to dinner at some point. I decided I would do dinner and then Uber home.

I came out, and he immediately asked if I wanted some mushrooms. I said no, then laughed in an attempt to make light of the increasingly awkward situation.

"I'm happy to start with dinner," I said. He laughed. *Okay, maybe he isn't a psychopath. Our IQs are not in the same range, though. At all.* I looked down in my cup of "magic water" and noticed some white and brown dust floating in it. Was it MDMA? GHB? Who the hell knew? He said it was superfood powder, but I felt uneasy and didn't touch the cup.

Now, why didn't I leave in this moment? Well, I was lonely. I yearned for attention and affection. And it felt exciting to take a risk. But under the desire for the high of a risk was a gaping hole in my heart, and I was attempting to distract myself from it.

The next thing I knew he was kissing me, and at that point, in my mind, I said yes to the affection. I had never been with a tall, six-pack-ab model type, and I needed to shift the internal narrative and remind myself that I had agency, that I was choosing this, that I could leave in any moment. But I was partially lying to myself and had lost contact with the feelings in my body and the truth of my heart. I actually had trouble leaving and saying no. So, to make myself feel better, I told myself that I was choosing it, but underneath there was a gap forming between me and my truth, and it was getting wider by the minute. Two things were happening at once: a desire for affection and a feeling that it was time to go.

That night he told me about his abusive childhood with his drug-addicted mother, the foster homes he'd lived in, his time in the war in Iraq and how he'd had to kill, and his life as a veteran. He spoke about how the wellness world had shunned him at times for being who he was, and at no point in his story could I tell what was real and what wasn't. I was lost in the labyrinth of my own stories. Was I enjoying this? Was I scared? Was I tough and cool? Was this okay? I didn't know. But in his stories of feeling like an outsider in the glitzy LA wellness world, I saw myself. I felt less alone when I saw us as two outsiders, two eccentrics, two hustlers trying to make it in LA. A bit wild, a bit fucked up, a bit unconventional.

When I got home the next day (yes, I slept on that terrible bed with unwashed sheets), I told all my girlfriends the story, and we laughed. To them, I was cool and tough and mystical, and I could handle things like that! But in order to handle that moment and the ones to come, I abandoned a tender, sensitive part of myself and put her in a box in the basement. She would cry to be heard, saying, "Please don't do this to me!" But I would ignore her with a too-cool-for-school mask of protection that rendered me untouchable by even the most lascivious moment with that man.

When he asked me out a second time after lots of loving text messages, sweet "good morning" notes, and kind calls, I thought, *Why am I being so hard on this guy? Maybe I am projecting my own fear of trusting men onto him. Maybe he didn't try to drug me or make a plan to seduce me instead of taking me to dinner. Maybe he's just a bit eccentric and has been through a lot.*

This was the "well, maybe" voice in action, the voice that tries to appease the intuition with rationality and facts but actually just abandons instincts and feeling altogether. My heart's shadow of hunger was leading the way, asking me to leave my intuition and truth, again. In that moment, I felt myself leave my center. So, when he asked, after all the sweet texts and calls, if I wanted to go to the hot springs with him on the full moon, I said to myself, *What's the harm?*

So I went against my inner knowing, and I blamed my lack of trust in men, my fear of intimacy, and my need to heal. As we exited town in his minivan on our way up the coast to the hot springs, on a night with a bright, full moon, he handed me his phone and said, "You have to watch this video. Have you seen it?" I held his phone in my lap and watched the POV-style video of someone murdering and raping people. At the end of the video, there was a reveal that the murderer was a woman. I told him I didn't want to keep watching, and he said, "You have to watch till the end. Don't be one of those LA people who is only light and love. Life is brutal. Watch the video." I deduced that he was angry at women and that he wanted me to see that women could be bad, too. But the whole thing made me sick to my stomach, and all of sudden, I realized I was in over my head. It was just a feeling, a deep knowing, that I now was paying full attention to. He then showed me bags of drugs in the backseat—a large bag of mushrooms and baggies of MDMA and some other bottles and vials. This was clearly a part of his business.

I told him I didn't feel well and asked if he could take me home. He said no. The wild thing was, a few hours before he picked me up, I had dropped my phone in the toilet, so it was sitting at home in a bowl of rice. I had no phone, and I was in a drug-filled minivan with a man I did not trust. What the hell was I thinking? He would not turn the car around no matter how much I explained my fake illness. So, at age thirty-three, I would repeat what I had done at age twenty-one when I went home with someone dark and dangerous despite the signs: I would spend the night pretending I was having fun and that I was okay until the man eventually took me back home.

Jumping out of a car on the Pacific Coast Highway with no phone at 8 pm was not an option. What would I do? I had made a bad choice, and I had to live with it. We went to the hot springs, the gap between me and my true self growing bigger and bigger as I continued to dissociate and abandon my truth. I knew how to stay calm, put on a smile, and lie. In the dark hot water pools, he kept trying to push his penis into my body, and to avoid conflict, I giggled and squirmed instead of shouting. Because I couldn't bear to be left in the woods alone with no phone and no one to help me, I decided to wait out the night and just get home. Throughout the night, I kept reminding myself that somewhere under his trauma, he was a good man. I tried to find that eternal child of God within him.

On the car ride home, he pushed my head into his lap and began to swerve, which caught the attention of a police officer, who pulled us over. I held my breath the entire time as I remembered the bags of drugs he had in the car. When the officer came over, he showed his smarts and pulled out his army ID, then said, "Oops, wrong ID. That's my army one." The cop immediately let him go, an unspoken pact.

I prayed to the heavens that night as the police officer pulled us over because I knew if he had gotten arrested with large amounts of drugs, I would have gone to jail, too. I wished I could have asked the officer for help, but I knew how those things went. I just had to get home.

Eventually, he dropped me off at home, and I was in shock. This time, I didn't tell anyone about it. I had said yes to him until I didn't. And then I said yes again to appease him. These moments are complex. I was not innocent. I had given all kinds of mixed signals. But I also had asked him to take me home, and he had said a very firm no. Like I said, these moments become like mazes when we self-abandon. They are very hard to get out of. I had gotten to that place because he was a flashy spiritual entrepreneur with 70K followers, a growing business, and a six-pack of chiseled abs, and I was excited and curious to date "spiritual" men in LA.

A few years later a group of women on Instagram called him out for being a rapist and a stalker. Many women stepped forward. I was approached by someone who knew I had gone out with him a few times, asking if I would share my story. At the time, I couldn't do it; the trauma of sharing it publicly was just too great. I said I would share privately as part of the case, but I don't know if it went anywhere. As far as I know, he is still out there with his ab pictures and superfoods. In the end, I cannot claim to be a victim; it is far too complex. But I can say I abandoned my truth, my intuition, and that those experiences were part of my heart's initiation into deep transformation and greater respect for what I feel. I now honor every little intuitive hit that I have.

How often do we choose to believe a lie instead of feeling the truth of the moment? Whatever feels seductive enough for us to abandon ourselves is just waiting, saying, "Come hither, baby . . ." and it can feel so easy to leave our center, leave the one inside who says, "Mayday, Mayday! Do not get into that car!"

Many of us feel our intuition every day, but we choose to ignore it. The way it communicates may not make sense in the same way the rational and linear parts of our psyche do, but intuition is a language of feeling that is as valid as any other language. We have weak spots where we don't see as clearly, where we are quicker to self-abandon, where we betray the boundaries we have set. Those weak spots are important to know. What do you desire so deeply that you would abandon your intuition to receive it? That you would lie to yourself to obtain it? Is it love, money, being seen, validation? We all have core wounds and hungers that aid us in bypassing our intuition, and it becomes our practice to know those weak spots, whether it's for ice cream, power, money, sex, fame, or love.

Your intuition is always speaking to you, telling you to stop, listen, and slow down, and we get to choose whether we listen or not. The times we don't listen can become our major teaching moments, moments of deep transformation, but these moments can also leave deep, painful scars that take a long time to heal. But when we have the courage to feel and notice what our body is saying, what our heart is whispering or shouting, even if it doesn't make sense, we strengthen the line of communication between ourselves and our truth. We have to dare to feel the scary whispers that tell us what we often don't want to hear. It may be as simple as saying, "Hmm, that just doesn't feel right," and not justifying why. People may not understand you, but you have to be willing to let go of needing their approval. In the end, you are the only one whose approval you need, your insides, your truth, your heart. It won't always make sense to people, and sometimes it means pissing people off or disrupting a moment. But ignoring your truth will always be more disruptive in the end.

Luckily, I did not get arrested that night—or worse. But the lies I told myself created emotional damage that I had to pay for in grieving and processing and learning to trust my own discernment, especially when it comes to men. After that lesson, though, I took more care, I listened more deeply, and eventually I was able to say yes to trustable men and listen when my body craved to say yes, but my deeper knowing said no.

Dare to Feel

REFLECTIONS

- How do your intuition and your heart speak to you? What sensations, feelings, or emotions let you know that these unseen parts are communicating with you?

- When was a time when you listened to the feelings in your body and used them to help you says "yes" or "no"?

- What painful heart initiations have you experienced that taught you to listen more closely to your feelings? What have you lost through ignoring them?

- Where has your desire for affection or love or intimacy eclipsed your common sense?

- Have you ever been intimate with someone you considered a "bad person" that you were later able to see was simply someone who was hurting? How did you make that shift in perspective?

RITUAL FOR FORGIVING SOMEONE WHO HURT YOU

Set your ritual space. Take some deep breaths. Consider a person whom you feel hurt by and feel your desire to forgive them. Make a donation to an organization the person you are longing to forgive would perhaps appreciate, and do it in honor of them. You can use their initials in the donation notes. You can say "in honor of," but make it clear to yourself that this is for them. This is an energetic token of your desire to be free of your anger or resentment toward them and to set them free. This is an offering that transcends words. Do not tell them. Let this be a private ritual between your soul and theirs, and an opportunity for your heart to soften and heal, even just a little.

IF SEX WERE CONSIDERED SACRED

If sex were like going to church,
what would you wear?
What scent would adorn you?
What words would be your prayer?

Hallelujah!
Praise the Lord!
Blessed Be!
Hail Mary!

What exclamations would be said while bodies
intertwined?

What sensations would be heightened
while hearts opened?

What tears would fall
as soul healing took place?

What devotion would pour forth
as you kneeled at the foot of love?

And then,
afterward,
would you go to brunch
to feast and celebrate,
the scent of prayer in the air,

your eyes locked onto your love,
your spiritual heart
exposed
for all to see
as you order your eggs
and sip coffee?

Soul shining,
amidst the mundane
world?

16

Creating New Relationships with Feeling Your Heart

Not every feeling needs to be acted on. Not every feeling needs to be given meaning. But feelings are not here to be ignored. They are like music from the universe that helps us recognize when something is off, or right and good, or alive and pulsing! Sometimes they can come from the unconscious and be completely unrelated to the present moment, and sometimes they are clues to present reality. Clues to leave a room. Clues to breathe more deeply. The universe is the cosmic DJ dishing out the emotional tunes, and we just dance.

But the problem is, a lot of us won't dance to the blues. We won't headbang to metal. I say this metaphorically, of course, but there is so much desire as a culture to only feel the good things that we miss the rich textures of sorrow, or the sharp edges of rage, or the heavy weight of shame. We want to skip over those parts so bad, and we find every way to distract ourselves. But, to paraphrase the words of author Francis Weller: What if we cultivate an apprenticeship with our sorrow? What if we sat and became curious? What if we undertook an apprenticeship with our shame? What if we became its student, taking notes, feeling the tones, sniffing it out, learning it, studying it?

We sometimes lack the ability to hold the sensations that come with emotions, so we dump them on to another person or bury them within ourselves. The sensations in the body that arise from grief, rage, heartbreak, loss, and confusion can lead to overwhelm. We were not taught how to feel in school, how to hold big energies in our bodies, how to breathe with big emotions, how to hold the energy when needed, then release it into tears and dancing and moaning and laughter. As children, we would perhaps just roll in fits of laughter whenever it came upon us, whenever the gods would have us laugh. And school told us to be quiet, because a room full of laughing kids would mean chaos! And so, the natural urge to laugh freely got wrung out of us. The big energy of joy became compressed and dampened for many of us. Joy holds massive sensation! Joy can be uncomfortable because it can be loud and disruptive! It is high energy, high sensation. Grief can also be big energy. If a wave of grief comes upon you, the room can feel like it's shaking or sinking, and your body can start to go through a response. To turn toward that level of sensation is brave.

Daring to live a life of deep feeling is not easy. We can get sucked into tunnels and black holes and feel like we can never get out. We feel too much, so we close. Most of us didn't have examples of elders holding circles for grief or singing songs of rage. We are removed from feeling what is happening on this planet. We stay "safe" within our bubbles and stay focused on the task at hand. To open to feeling would be messy and scary. What if too much dark arises? What if it won't go away? What if we open to feel and feel so much existential pain that we are paralyzed? There are risks in daring to feel, in daring to open the heart to the massive experience of life on this planet. When we feel, we notice where we are impacting others, where we are hurting those we love. When we feel, more empathy is possible, and within a more empathetic culture, we are less separate, less private, and less ashamed. But it can feel like a gauntlet to cross, to be able to open to the storm within when it comes, to learn the skills needed to calm and soothe and self-regulate and ask for help and not drown in the open sea of feeling.

As we've learned, there are many different types of feelers. There are those who avoid feeling at all costs: perhaps a tear slips out here and there in the darkness of a movie theater, but they mostly don't cry. They mostly keep at their missions and stay out of the feeling. There are those who are always drowning in feeling. They feel like an Italian opera, and there is a need for more regulation and to work on that "feeling valve." Perhaps they are addicted to the theater of feeling but haven't landed in the heart underneath it all. There are those feelers who are okay with feeling good, happy, and joyful, but feeling rage, grief, or deep sorrow, especially in community, is a mighty edge. There are those who are not open to feel at all, their hearts seemingly permanently closed from pain or trauma, and it may take a Mack Truck of drugs or alcohol for them to crack. And there are the pretenders who feign that they are "good," but two layers down they are not, and eventually it starts to show. Perhaps they only give themselves permission to feel in therapy, or in private. Then there are those who are trying to find a regulated middle road of heart opening and closing, like a butterfly's wings opening and shutting as they breathe and rest. These folks want to feel the wider world, then the personal, then pause and notice it all.

The list goes on, and we often shift what kind of feeler we are based on our life circumstances. We are free to feeler hop, and no feeler is wrong. It's just a journey of noticing where we are and how open or closed we are to life.

Sometimes on the journey of feeling we can go from stuffing in all our feelings or being numb to feeling anything and everything, and when we learn to feel again, it is like an ocean that is unbridled and comes through with an air of entitlement. After all the years of not feeling, we basically have a debutante ball for each feeling, and it can be a bit embarrassing when we look back. We see that we paraded each feeling around, like, "Here I am, feeling so sad, and it is my birthright!" And of course, IT IS. But over time as we get into a juicy relationship with our feelings, sensations, and emotions, we won't need to parade each one in public. In fact, many of them become private, and we turn toward them internally, feel them, love them, and let the wave of them wash through us and be released. But intimacy teaches us that many can be shared within our communities and families.

You could see something online that brings up the feeling of unworthiness, and it hits in your heart. You may think, "That person is worthy of money and love and success, and I am not." You follow the feeling of sinking dread and blue sadness, and it starts to possess you and take hold of you, and after a while you no longer remember why you feel so awful. Or you could see a picture that brings up your feelings of unworthiness and sit with the part of you that feels unworthy, give her a moment to feel that pain with some breaths and maybe journaling or crying or shouting to a song, then come back to the present moment and notice the beauty around you. In this moment of looking around you and noticing your life, you see what *is* working, what you *are* worthy of, even if it's simple. A hot meal. The sun. A good book. You train yourself to feel the beauty in the small things, too.

This is not the same as the cliché of "look on the bright side," but try your best not to get into the habit of following every feeling and then letting it possess you for hours or days. There are times when we need to give a feeling space and times when we don't need to go there because it's actually a pattern, or an addiction, or a way of avoiding our lives. If you discern that is the case and that the feeling has been felt, take a cold shower, put on a dance song, or call a friend. **Strike a healthy balance between avoiding and denying a feeling and letting it possess you and dictate how you experience your whole life. Underneath all of it is love, and to get there we must dare to feel.**

Dare *to* Feel

REFLECTIONS

Spend some time contemplating what type of feeler you are.
Circle which applies to you:

- Over-empathetic and unboundaried . . .   yes   no   sometimes
- High drama . . .   yes   no   sometimes
- Always cool and calm . . .   yes   no   sometimes
- Tough exterior, never shows emotions . . .   yes   no   sometimes
- Good vibes only . . .   yes   no   sometimes
- Addicted to the blues . . .   yes   no   sometimes
- Feeling everyone else's feelings but
  not my own . . .   yes   no   sometimes
- Sunsets always make me cry . . .   yes   no   sometimes
- Hard to find the wonder in life . . .   yes   no   sometimes
- Laugh often but don't cry often . . .   yes   no   sometimes
- Cry often but don't laugh often . . .   yes   no   sometimes

Have a look at this list and reflect on the type of feeler that you are at this time in your life. What do you notice? Where could you use a little more time or awareness or feeling? What could you use less of? Assess with love. Return to this in six months and see if the way you feel has changed.

RITUAL FOR LIBERATING FEELING

Close your bedroom door. Light a candle. Sit in front of the mirror. Take the list above and try to feel each type of feeler in your body. Embody each one and allow yourself to get dramatic. Call forth your inner actor and artist, make sounds, jump around. See which feels the silliest, which fits easily, and which feels alien to you. Try on each feeler as deeply as you can. Does one that doesn't feel like "you" actually feel liberating to embody? You can use music to help you get deeper into each character if you like. Then shake it out and let them go.

TYPES OF FEELERS

There are many types of feelers running around this world.

There is the "I feel everything, and it overwhelms me,
and I am an empath,
and it's terrifying to feel so much,
and I need more boundaries, and that is my job this life"
feeler.

And the "I feel nothing,
and I never have,
and I just don't feel a lot,
and the good feels okay,
and the bad feels okay,
but I don't cry much,
and I wish I did sometimes,
and I would like to feel more,
but this is how I am"
feeler.

The "I shut down 'cause things were too hard as a kid
and now I don't feel"
feeler.

The "I used to hold it all in
and smile
and be pretty and sweet,
and now I feel things and it's insane
and I don't know where to put all these feelings"
feeler.

The "I love to feel joy
and I feel a lot of happy things,
but I don't feel much pain
or grief and anger
and I am scared of those things"
feeler.

The "I feel so much sadness and grief all the time
at this world,
but joy is always out of reach"
feeler.

The "I feel everyone else's feelings
but not my own"
feeler.

The "too cool for feelings"
feeler.

The "too busy for feelings"
feeler.

The "I have worked hard to feel my feelings in real time
and also to not get stuck in each wave
or give it meaning
and to discern which feelings are mine
and the feelings of others
and also when the feeling is old
and needs attention

but has no relation to the present
and how to feel
without hot potato-ing
the feeling
onto
another"
feeler.

This is the feeler I aspire to be.

Feeling Again After Shutting It All Down to Survive

Feeling it all is not just feeling emotions and sensations, but simply feeling your life! Feeling the sun on your face, feeling empathy for the unhoused person you pass on the street, feeling how music dances in your body, and feeling the love and emptiness that sit within the ground of your being. When we shut down feeling, we shut down the good stuff, the alive stuff, and we rob ourselves of life. And we don't consciously do the shutting down; it is usually trauma or societal conditions. But slowly, or quickly, we shut down all feeling because we sense it isn't safe to feel; life doesn't feel safe, so we don't feel safe in our bodies. We build a wall against feeling life. Some walls are built from hot fire that throws a burning dart at you to back away if you get too close. Have you met those people who have a fire wall? Again, it's probably not their fault. They were likely hurt, and that wall protects them, but behind the wall there is usually a little one needing a hug.

And then there are the ice wallers, those who've built an ice castle around them to feel safe. You could be in the middle of sharing your heart with them, and you'll notice that they get an empty look in their eyes, and suddenly you know: *They are not here anymore. They went into the ice castle.* Ice castle people don't usually throw fire darts, though some people do both. In my twenties I had nailed the role of Ice Queen. My boyfriend would go into a rage as I went into cold, nonresponsive

Ice-Queen mode. She was a handy defense I had built when my child-hood felt unsafe: "If I seem unaffected, I am fine." But I also got good at throwing fire darts from behind the ice wall when someone was least expecting it. Behind these fire and ice walls, though, was a little girl with a halo of curls and big teardrops dripping down her cotton shirt. She was so lonely, so scared. She needed someone stable to care for her, and she didn't always get that, but it took me a while to get to her and see that she was there underneath all my defenses.

There are so many ways besides fire and ice that we consciously or unconsciously shut down feeling. Consciously shutting down could look like watching hours of *The Kardashians* because you have felt your sad heart all day and you need an effing break. And unconsciously shut-ting down could look like spacing out and going void mid-conversation with your partner because their message feels overwhelming. You may accidentally emotionally abandon the moment as your presence leaves them and what they are saying, and/or yourself, as you space out and exit your body. You may not be sure exactly where you go, but you may tend to end up in your own ice castle, where it feels safer. You may not even know you are doing it, and you may like to think no one will notice, but then you learn that those around you feel lonely in your presence when you do it.

Most people walk through life not knowing they are shutting down or checking out. Even the ones who deeply cling to another to "survive" are turning away from themselves, which is a form of shutting down. Survival is key, and shutting down helps us survive. It's like closing the valve on feeling and saying, "I'm full, thank you." The thing is, many of us learn to do this as children, and when we start to feel safer as adults, we don't know how to open the "I want to feel life" valve again. And so it takes WAY more stimulus to feel something. More action movies. More booze. More loud music. More sex. Louder, faster, stronger, and BOOM, *then* we can feel. But we may not notice the small things—the sounds of birds or the person on the street who needs help—so checking in with your own life-feeling valve is key! And then you can start to work with ways to open it gently.

There are those of us who feel so much because our feeling valve doesn't exist! Our feelings are so overwhelming that our walls are the only way we know how to make a boundary from feeling more. Some people have only two feeling modes: all the way open and all the way closed. But it's ideal to have a valve that has all the in-between spots on the spectrum, too. Because it doesn't work to be wide open all the time, or closed and shored up all the time. There are times when it is appropriate to feel less. There are moments when we are at full capacity and feeling more could be harmful. The ping-pong, back-and-forth swing of extremes is another lack of emotional health. **Walking the middle path, where we dare to feel but also dare to hold flexible boundaries, and pause, and discern what we are available for in any given moment, is a harder path.** It requires more awareness of our patterns to know if we are closing our feeling valve because we are truly reaching capacity, or because we are avoiding feeling something important. Feeling can seem inconvenient, and it's up to us to learn how to integrate a practice of daring to feel into our lives so we feel each other, so we feel the truth of the moment and stay connected to this world.

One way people open the valve up quickly can be with drugs, plant medicines, or psychedelics. Many people with PTSD or severe trauma may need to call in the big power helpers to get the feeling self back online, and substances like MDMA, psilocybin, and ayahuasca can really help with that. People who haven't cried in years are suddenly able to cry again. People who can't usually feel things like empathy and subtle contentment begin to notice life's sensations more closely. For some people, that is just way too much feeling at once! In those cases, weekly therapy, somatic work, art therapy, and embodiment practices can help build a stable, consistent relationship with the feeling valve and in turn a deeper relationship, or a new one, with their soul. **When the feeling valve is closed off, it is impossible to live close to one's soul.** And so, the steps of opening again and again become steps to feeling a soul reunion with the depths of your being.

There are many good reasons to unwind the defenses and open the feeling valve slowly and carefully, because if you open it too much, too fast, you can actually create more harm for yourself and those around you. I've seen this happen with plant medicine and breathwork. As you do this healing work, it is very important that you listen to your intuition, and if you can't find it, ask for help from a loving, trusted guide who is attuned to you and has your best interest at heart.

I am not a scientist or a therapist, but I am a devoted practitioner, teacher, and guide who has healed from habitual shutdowns, from feeling too much, and from a lack of emotional boundaries. Over the last twenty years, I have come to a place of safe, trustable feeling by utilizing a combo of the big stuff, like walking into fire, and small stuff, like daily writing and learning to feel my heart. The most important thing about the process of feeling and creating a healthy feeling valve is PATIENCE. It *will* take time, and there may be numb days where you just want to reach for a stimulus, like sugar, crazy TV, video games, or a glass of wine. And that is okay, but only if you keep trying and you keep coming back to feeling. Over time, you may even ask yourself, "Did that bag of M&M's bring me into my heart? Did its sweetness open me to life?" And maybe the answer is yes! And some days the answer may be no. Either way, it's okay. Go slow and breathe. Don't judge yourself, or at least, try not to.

When I think of the many healing curriculums or assignments that life has to offer, learning to feel again with healthy titration of the feeling valve is a beautiful one. The shutdowns may have come from unimaginable horrors, but the journey to reopen the heart and feel music, love, empathy, compassion, sorrow, poetry, the touch of a friend, and the magic of the moonlight is such a beautiful one. It's just that a lot of people are scared to go on the journey, and rightly so. How do we deal with the grief and rage that come up when we start to open again? It can be intense. That is why taking it slow is so great. If you asked me for advice on this five years ago, I would have said, "Go hard! Go fast! Get in there!" But now I say, "Take it slow. Go at your own pace. Make space for the grief and pain that arise as you feel again."

As you move forward on this journey, you will get more and more used to working with the big feelings that arise instead of cutting them out of your days. Yes, some midday grief while you have lunch is "inconvenient," but if you smoosh it down, where does it go? Could you give it three minutes of your time with some breath and a few sighs or sobs? If you're in the car with your kids and some rage about the past comes up, could you turn on a song and suggest you all do a primal scream together, then laugh afterward?

From here, you can live with an open heart again. You can live close to the truth of who you are. This feels like home. This feels like love. Even on hard days, you know you are close to the truth of who you really are. You trust it's part of your journey. This is where we accept all of life's ups and downs as material on the path. We stop fighting suffering and uncertainty, and we learn to be patient and cultivate love and compassion for ourselves and others in hard times and good times. We leave the past and begin to live in the present.

Dare *to* Feel

REFLECTIONS

- When do you build a wall between yourself and feeling? When people yell? When you feel scared? Attacked? Embarrassed? Do you have a habit of ever going icy cold?

- Do you ever overheat with anger or rage? How does your anger come out toward others? Bitterness? Spite? Direct aggression? Name calling? Shouting?

- What do you do when you are full up on feeling and need to empty a bit?

- What does it feel like when you close off to life and to those you love?

- Do you ever space out mid-conversation when you feel overwhelmed? When was the last time you did?

- What is your favorite way to "check out" of too much feeling?

- What opens your heart and feeling valve again after they close?

RITUAL FOR OPENING TO FEELING

Create and set your ritual space. Choose two songs that are angry and intense and raucous and ragey. Then choose two songs that usually make you cry, be they love songs or sad songs. Lie on a yoga mat with a blanket covering you and make sure you feel safe to make some noise. Use a sound machine for privacy, or wait until no one is home. Play the angry songs and use your breath to make some sounds. You can punch a pillow, or groan, yell "Haaaa," or simply scream. Take it slow. Do not push too hard.

Then, as the sad songs come on, put your hands on your heart and begin to make sounds. Try making crying sounds or any sound that feels cathartic! Even if it doesn't feel natural, try it. Make the sounds of guttural sobs and moans. Tell your body it is safe to feel. Even if you end up feeling just a little bit, that is great. Use this ritual for opening to feeling anytime you feel emotionally stuck or you need to turn the feeling valve back on and open your heart again to life.

THE PATH TO HEART LIBERATION

The path to liberation of the heart
is the path of walking through roses
with spiky thorns
and drips of honey
laced with poison,
where the poison is the medicine
and the medicine is the poison,
and the flower that you sniff sweetly with glee
is also the one that will unravel you to tears.
That is the way this world was built.
For every treasure,
there is a matching terror.
For every gain,
a matching loss.
And you just walk on,
you don't stop loving and opening
because of a loss or grievance;
you let your heart feel them,
but you keep on
walking the path of heart liberation.

Otherwise, you could get stuck along that path,
falling into fear,
running from Love,
stopping and licking the poisoned honey drip
of complaint or judgment,
of never enough,
and closing off to all of it,
joining the souls writhing in pain,
stuck in fear,
afraid of Love.
You might reach out a hand,
stay and sing a song,
and wipe a tear from where bellies
lie face down upon the earth,
deep in the forgetting of Love.
Take good care.
You may get sucked into
suffering
that leaves you bare!
But if you stay close to Love,
even in dark lands,
you can stop for a short caress,
leave a glass of water,
and then keep walking
along the path,
tears streaming down your heart walls
and laughter echoing through your halls.
When the vines of the fears grip at your ankles,
you can let them enter you,
but stay open,
stay close to the heart . . .
Hold those fear babies gently and guide them home.
Leave them a rose and a prayer
and walk ahead on the Path of Love . . .

Opening
Loving
Feeling
Staying here and now
In this body,
Heart Open.

PART 3

AWAKENING TO THE OPENHEARTED WAY

18

The Innocent Heart

D o you like me? Check yes or no," I slyly wrote on a piece of notebook paper as my second-grade teacher talked about gerunds. My red nails were chipped and dotted with a soul-revealing glitter sheen.

"If yes, will you kiss me?" I added, before passing the note two desks to the right to Matt Miller, who was wearing a T-shirt with a T. rex on it, his light brown hair trimmed neatly in a crew cut. Oh, the audacity of eight-year-old me who rocked wild curls that fell over my face as I brazenly asked for what I wanted in my bright pink cotton tee that had begun to pill from too many washes.

To my surprise, he checked "yes" and shoved the note back into my tiny hand in the cafeteria that day, the fluorescent lights above illuminating my virgin skin as I tingled with the high of connection, affection, and attention. I abandoned the faded tangerine-colored plastic tray that held limp green beans and a tiny carton of milk and rushed into a bathroom stall to open the note, pressing it to my chest. Mischief coursed through my body as I breathed a sigh of relief.

To be liked by someone!

I'm not sure where I found the courage or inspiration to ask for love and affection in that bold way. I was just a kid in Marietta, Georgia, growing up amidst Presbyterian churchgoers and soccer moms with sun-spotted legs and souped-up minivans. But I was curious and brave.

I'd had a boyfriend in kindergarten named Anthony, an ongoing flirt with the next-door neighbor, Carlos Mañuel, and even some harmless flirtations with my boy cousins in Brazil. Unconsciously or consciously, I was already feeling the pull of romantic connection from within my being. I was on my way to getting hooked on the allure of it. The magic of connection made me feel like I had swallowed stars that lit me up from the inside, creating an effervescent dazzle under my skin and a warm honey glow in my belly.

Matt Miller came over to my house that weekend for a playdate. I took him into the woods behind our Cape Cod–style cottage, looked at him, and said, "Are you gonna do it?" At first he pretended he didn't remember, but a soft rose blush spread across his cheeks, calling his bluff. Pine needles crunched underfoot, and the possibility of disturbing a copperhead snake amidst the brush only added to the magic of the moment. Then he quickly kissed me on the cheek, the sun peeking low at us through fuzzy pine trees, and he rushed back into the house before his mother, with her perfectly coiffed crimson hair, came to pick him up.

A portal opened within my chest that day, a breath of freedom in my tiny body that had stumbled on a natural antidote to the pain, confusion, and fear of living—connection, risk, feeling, freedom, love. Sometimes it is not about healing or going deep into the grief, rage, sorrow, or sadness. Sometimes it is about creating another door, not to escape, but to let Love enter at any moment and expand us. It doesn't make all the pain go away forever, but it asks us to open to life, to the moment, to another person, and with that opening, we feel released from the density of life and called into a soaring feeling of relief.

When love is present, we're more resilient to the pain. We feel hope; we feel held. Be it friend love, pet love, or any kind of love. Innately we know that connection is the antidote to pain, yet many of us are conditioned to muscle our way through things and tackle them solo. Living in an individualistic culture means many of us just deal with things on our own. Our instinct to reach out and ask for help, a hug, a friend, has been broken. But if we look back to when we were kids, likely we were not ashamed (at least at first) to ask for connection when we were hurting. **Awakening our heart is both a return to innocence and a maturation.**

Dare to Feel

REFLECTIONS

- When have you let yourself deeply enjoy the magic of connection? What conditions allowed this to happen, and how did it feel?

- How comfortable are you to ask for the connection you want? Bring to mind a time when you wanted to connect more deeply, but you held back. What stopped you?

- How willing are you to risk looking silly to fulfill your desires? Can you think of a time when you took this risk and got exactly what you wanted? How did it feel?

- Does your walk upon the transformational path of the heart include a bit of romance and devotion to love and possibility? What calls forth that romantic possibility for you?

RITUAL FOR CONNECTION

Take a risk on connection today. Make eyes with a stranger on a train or in a café. Smile at someone. Make a new gesture for your Beloved that you aren't sure if they will like—perhaps dressing in a new way for them or cooking them something new. Text an old friend you fell out of touch with. Respond to an email from a person you have been avoiding. Find one act that feels risky enough for you that you would almost rather not do it, and make this an emblematic moment of remembering who you are and how magical your life can be when you dare to feel. Notice the feelings that come up as you engage in this act, and try to give each one a name.

EARTH ANGELS

I said, "Maybe we should get matching tattoos that say Earth Angels."

(I meant, "Somehow we managed to find each other in this vast, crazy human realm, and we mustn't forget our mission: to love!")

You said, "Funny. I accidentally carved a candle that said Earth Angel on it last week."

(I thought, "The mission of souls who came to love always shines through!")

You said, "Thank heavens we found each other here and don't have to do it alone."

RISK IT FOR LOVE

I will not live small.
I have never been afraid to give love a try.
Why would I stop now?

19

Fearless Feeling and Self-Trust

As I waited for my oat latté at an LA café, I couldn't help but notice that everyone I saw had their necks craned down as their attention dissolved into a small screen. I mean, can it even be called a phone at that point? It is a *world*. A world outside of the coffee-scented café that offered a light remix of a Brazilian bossa nova in the background and a warm breeze from the open door. So much to feel. But it felt like I was the only one there . . . like really *there*. Everyone else seemed like they had fallen into the black hole of smartphone screens, vacant and disembodied. Were they feeling the beauty of this moment?

When I consider how we got here, I remember the '80s and '90s, a time when our offline lives were still more enticing, glamorous, wild, and weird than what the online worlds could offer. No matter that you could chat sexy-like on AIM for hours with strangers, there was still an enchantment to real life that nothing could match. A finger skimming the waistline between your shirt and jeans, the feeling of a tongue touching another's, a whisper tickling the inside of your ear. And cafés had people in them who read books and papers and chatted with each other. People looked out of windows and daydreamed, said hello to each other; our necks were still intact and our eyes were still fixed on the possibility of finding a date *in the room*.

Part of my own unofficial, self-imposed training as a woman on a mystical path involved traveling around the world with no phone and no plan. Nothing trained my intuition like traipsing through the streets of Rome or a small town in Brazil with no way of knowing if I was going in the right direction. This uncertainty propelled me to ask strangers for help again and again and learn to trust my intuition more than anything. Moments of connection turned into dinner invitations, long conversations on the bus, flirting in the streets, sometimes tears on the side of a dark road and heart-thumping anxiety, but always real, tangible, blood-and-bones moments that will never be forgotten.

My whole being was open for connection as I walked through the streets of Vienna or Venice with my 35 mm Canon camera around my neck, snapping photos of whomever I pleased. I had no fear when I asked people for directions or how to say this or that in Italian or French or German or Czech. I developed character and grit as I hopped on and off trains and buses, fielded gropes from strange men, and scribbled in my journal while sitting on the steps of the cathedral at Chartres.

One of my earliest memories of learning to trust my intuition and living life fully happened on a weekend trip to Genova. Who goes to Genova? I'm not sure, but I picked it on the map. Out of all of Italy's magical and medieval cities, it wasn't much to write home about, but I had a feeling I needed to go. At nineteen years old, I had joined an organization called Servas International. It was a pre–couch surfing deal where you could stay with people across the world. You had to interview to get in, and it was aimed to promote cross-cultural exchange. I interviewed in the home of a middle-aged man who lived in the East Village. I felt no fear going to this man's apartment on 4th and D and chatting him up while seated on his faded blue couch. He approved me as a member, and I got a book listing all the willing hosts from the countries I would be visiting.

Two months later, I flipped through Genova's host book from my room in Florence, looking for a host family with kids my age and similar interests, since hobbies were listed in the guidebook. I landed on a family with a son my age and a daughter a few years younger. I emailed them from the clunky desktop at my school in Florence, and the mother said her son would meet me at the train station if he was able. I worried a bit. *How will I know where to meet him? How will I know if it is him? How long should I wait?* I surrendered and hoped for the best, living a pre-smartphone and -laptop life.

I wore a turban over my hair made from the old curtains that used to line my lofted bed in my shitty-but-artsy Avenue B apartment. The fabric was a mint green gauze, and I had taken to wrapping it around my head in some yogi-inspired kind of way. I had big shell earrings dangling from my ears and black cotton Mary Jane's from Chinatown on my feet with black ballet pants under a black dress. This was my daily uniform.

Outside the train station, Pietro waited for me on a white 1969 Vespa. How did I know it was him? I just did. How did I fit the helmet over my DIY turban headpiece? I cannot tell you. But I did. We zoomed through the streets of Genova, and I experienced a sort of ecstasy I had never felt before. It was the feeling of complete freedom, inside and outside. *No one in the whole world knows where I am.* I was on the back of a bike in a country where I didn't know anyone. I had no one to text. Or email. No DMs waiting for me. No smartphone. No maps. I was free. Perhaps it's cliché, but does it matter? We never know if we will again feel the liberation we once tasted in youth, so what is the problem with celebrating and longing for it again?

Pietro got me to the apartment safely, where his mom and her partner made us pasta with bright green nutty pesto. Pietro disappeared into the background of the room and didn't eat with us. Later I heard the front door slam, and he was gone. His sister was away, and his mother and her partner were leaving to go out of town the next morning. So, he and I would be there alone for the weekend. They gave me blankets to make my nights on the couch comfortable, a key to use, and a map to get around town. Perhaps they wondered what a twenty-year-old girl was doing in Genova alone. Why was I not traveling with university friends? Why Genova and not someplace more scenic like Cinque Terre or Venice?

Well, I was alone because I was good at being alone. And as far as I could tell, the other kids in the NYU Florence program weren't in art school at Tisch like I was, and I didn't feel I had much in common with them.

There were also kids from Duke in the program, and they felt even more foreign, wearing khakis and baseball caps. I had chosen the most "basic" of study abroad programs, and I did it on purpose. I could have stayed with the art school kids in Paris or London or Prague, but I was drawn to the most clichéd and iconic place to visit: Florence. Later I would find out why: in Florence, I would meet the spiritual community of yogis and monastics that would forever change my path. But that revelation wouldn't present itself for a few more weeks. Regardless, my intuition was spot-on without Google and Instagram to cloud its potency. I was running off of Source and pure soul-knowing.

I walked around Genova, took a ferry, had lunch, and went into a museum. I thought the city was quite plain for an Italian city, and I quickly felt a lonely melancholy that I was strangely accustomed to. By the time I got back to the apartment it was dusk, and all was quiet. There was no internet to keep me company, no apps, and no way to correspond with folks back home. Just quiet. I sat on the slick black leather couch in the living room while the sun set and darkness fell around me. There was nothing to do but sit there in the dark and be. I heard the door open and in walked Pietro, his tall, thin frame hanging quietly in the dark. He was clearly a stoic, present and emotionless. He looked at me with little expression on his face and asked, "Do you want to come to a party with me?"

"Yes," I replied.

"Great, let's go."

He loaned me a hoodie of his even though we were still wrapped in the warmth of early September. He said it might be cold where we were going.

We got on the back of his 1969 Vespa and catapulted our bodies into the night, riding up and up and up into the mountains. The temperature dropped quickly, it was pitch black out, and I was in heaven. I had no backpack, no water, no snacks, no map, no smartphone; it was just Pietro, me, and the black of night.

Several hours later, we arrived at a thick dark forest under a moonless sky, and EDM blasted from big, stacked speakers as bodies mingled like moving shadows. Pietro looked at me and said, "Have fun," then wandered off, becoming just another apparition in a sea of gray shapes. It was an Italian punk anarchist rave, and I stood out like a sore thumb in the hoodie and my turban. I was left standing in the black forest alone, but it didn't matter. I didn't have water. But it didn't matter. I was not drinking or on drugs, but it didn't matter.

That night, I found myself in a ceremony of rebirth into freedom. I was an adult, no longer living in my mother's home in Marietta, Georgia, no longer bound to the church, the southern good girl persona I was given, or the social norms of my little suburban life. That night, I cut the first layer of cords from my parents, traumas, beliefs, and implanted future visions. That was my first weekend in Italy, my first weekend living free as an adult.

Alone in the dark forest among many bodies, I did not try to get to know people. The music was so loud, I barely spoke any Italian, and it was pitch black, so I went into my own heart, my inner world, and I was met by my breath, my courage, my bare soul. At twenty years old, I was like a baby being born to sounds of bass and beats in a dark void, a liminal space where creation itself pushed out something new. I was in the womb of the Goddess, and I couldn't feel better being there. I danced all night and prayed to Her. To Life. To the Great Mystery. The whole night was a cleansing of everything I knew, and as the hours went by, I stayed alone. No one knew where I was, and I did not know where Pietro was. No one in the world was tracking me. I was truly free in that tar-black forest of the Apennine, surrounded by strangers. Everything I thought of as "me" slipped away, and I was no one, completely alone. It was almost as if Alexandra no longer existed. I just was. Mush. Void. Womb. Pre-life. Post-me.

I danced and prayed and sat in meditation upon the earth that night until the sun rose. My feet were cold, and no one had come to speak with me all night, which felt quite rare. I'm not sure if they noticed I was in my own ceremony, or if I looked out of place, or if perhaps I had made myself energetically invisible. Perhaps I was between personas and simply did not exist. As the sun rose, I looked up from where I was sitting and saw Pietro standing there, like my Zen teacher coming to fetch me after sending me up the mountain to meditate alone with my inner ghosts.

He calmly asked, "Are you ready to go?"

"Yes," I said, and I stood up, my Bambi legs shaky and new. We walked to the Vespa in silence. It was a moment beyond words. Dawn was being born, and we were its witnesses.

We began to ride down the mountain as the sun crested pink over the trees and the rain began to fall. We pulled the Vespa over and sat in a shelter on the side of the road with an old hunter and his hound as he smoked a cigar. We still didn't say a word. We just sat in silence together, watching the sky change colors, from deep blue to soft purple to blush pink as the rain fell around us. Is this birth? My heart was the sky now, changing colors, dripping, opening, and releasing things I didn't have language for. I was in a great dialogue beyond words with those hills, the sky, the smoke, the hound, Pietro, Italy. My edges were melting into all of it.

It was too slippery to ride down the mountain, so Pietro hid the bike, and we stood on the road and thumbed a ride down to Genova. When we got back to his apartment, we barely spoke. I took a portrait of him on black-and-white film, a portrait I will never forget. The look in his eyes was piercing and deep and spoke to worlds beyond this one. Later that day, I took a taxi back to the train station and said goodbye. We exchanged a few letters after that, and I sent the portrait along with a painting of his eyes to him. It was not about romance. It was just about living fully alive. Free. In the moment. Trusting life.

Back in LA, in the crowded café, I wondered if the freedom before smartphones, that feeling in the chest of wide-open sky and pink clouds sucking on my skin, would ever return. As folks' heads bowed down into their small black boxes, I wondered if they saw the two-year-old giggling wildly while his Mama tickled him, her latté nearly spilling. Or the old man whose face told story after story upon wrinkle after wrinkle as he waited to be asked about his time in the war or when he immigrated here from his childhood home. As the roses on the counter opened their petals as if to brag, did they cry as busy customers rushed in and out, texting and tapping and scrolling? Will the Real beg us or force us back down and into her? Only time will tell. Perhaps it is simple, as simple as leaving the phone at home, wandering into a walk, saying hello to a stranger, saying yes, and choosing life, here and now.

In today's ever-busier world, when do we stop to enjoy and deeply feel the details of life? How brave is it to put down the phone and just be with what we feel? The moment is waiting for you with its magic, but how will you see it if you are buried in your phone? It is incredibly brave to leave your phone in your bag or pocket and be in public without it as a safety blanket. To just observe. To simply be open. To meet the eyes of a stranger or strike up a conversation. We feel so much more of life this way. Life's riches are waiting to melt into us—the elements, the sounds, the scenes, the synchronicities. But the phone or screen can often interrupt that transmission. Our humanity is in our bodies where all the juicy feelings are, where the heart is—not on a screen, not on Google or Instagram. Though connection and feeling can happen online, it is controlled, small, temporal, and often not fully true. There is more space for projection and lies and false stories. Skin to skin, face to face, there is more space for honesty, openness, sensation.

This is your life. You get to choose how you live it. Will you experience all of it through the lens of Instagram or Facebook or TikTok, or will you experience it through your body and heart first? Will you dare to live in the present, in your own skin, or choose to live through screens? This is your choice. To feel, here and now, and let each moment deeply in, as your deepest soul food, or not.

Dare *to* Feel

REFLECTIONS

- When was the last time you went a day (or a few hours) without screens? What inspired you to do this?

- How did it feel? Was it weird to not be tethered to your phone? Did you feel lonely or disconnected? Did that ever shift into a feeling of freedom or aliveness?

- When do you feel most alive, in general? Does feeling fully alive feel expansive in your chest? Or belly? Do you feel taller? More whimsical? More wild? More electric? More inspired? More free?

- What memories do you have of feeling totally free? Reflect on these, from when you were a child to now. What were the smells and tastes and sounds of that time? Who were you with? Paint the scenes for yourself.

RITUAL FOR PAUSING SCREEN TIME

Choose a day to spend without your phone. Carry a book, a journal, or art supplies wherever you go, and in any moment when you would usually reach for your phone, notice what feelings are present for you. Throughout the day, take a moment to look up, make eye contact with someone, or ask someone a question. Take a walk or sit in the park and watch the dogs play. If you get "bored," notice what feelings are underneath your boredom. Journal or draw them. Stare at the ocean or the sunset. Let your mind wander. Notice if your imagination feels more active, and jot down any ideas in a journal. Close the day by cooking a meal while listening to your favorite music. What feels different in your body? If you enjoy this ritual, extend it to a whole weekend. Or commit to taking a daily walk with no phone.

HOW TO FEEL ALIVE

Imagine eyes as healing beams of light.

Let love ooze through your pores when you sweat,
be generous with glances, smiles, money, and words!

Arrive at each moment as if meeting with the Divine.
Laugh at inner demons, and tickle them, and hug them!

Let roses be role models.
Be considerate to Earth, thank trees!
Imagine someone yummy is licking your neck at least once a day.
Eat food like you're making love to it.
Apply empathy, liberally and widely.
Feel the Divine's hand on your lower back at all times.

Listen to samba and dancehall music,
and gently move your hips while in the subway or on the bus.

Get on your knees and kiss the floor
or your hands
or your feet
every day
as thanks for the gift of being alive!

Talk to statues on your altar like besties via text.
And love life.

I dare you.

Turning toward Love, Especially When It Hurts

When my mom got out of the mental hospital after her breakdown, she had lost everything. It wasn't her fault. The system just isn't set up to support people going through hard times. When people get sick and bills get delayed, the government is quick to yell "foreclosure" and offer bankruptcy as a solution. So as my mom took time off to heal, she lost our cute Cape Cod–style cottage of a home in Georgia with its bay windows in the kitchen, big wooden swing on the porch, and my room with its sky-blue ceiling and painted wispy clouds I would stare at as I fell asleep. First came her divorce, then she got sick, lost her job, lost her home, filed for bankruptcy, and then came the full breakdown. Like dominos falling, one by one. Who wouldn't feel like giving up after all that loss? Losing a house meant leaving behind home, safety, security, our roots, and, for me, memories, like first kisses and first sex and getting ready for dance recitals and the prom. We scooped up as many memories as we could in recycled boxes sealed with twisted packing tape. Boxes filled with pointe shoes and corsages and crumpled love notes now lived in a storage unit in Talladega, Florida, tucked into the wet panhandle near Panama City, far from their original home, waiting, soft in their sleep.

Even though my mom and stepdad were divorced during this painful and messy time, because she had lost everything she owned, he offered for her to live in a trailer he owned that was parked in a vacation trailer community in southern Alabama. I didn't see her for over a year while she was in the hospital as I was scared, nervous, and didn't know how to deal with what was happening to her. Things had gotten complex; she needed space, and I needed space. Boundaries were too soft and I was trying to become an adult, but it felt like time to show up. My girlfriend, Noa, the Israeli, eccentric, artist soul, volunteered to come with.

"Alabama sounds like a film I would love to watch. Will we go to a football game or shoot guns?" she asked cheekily in her thick accent while sipping a crisp white in our Greenpoint Brooklyn apartment as the sun set over the Brooklyn Queens Expressway, which we could see from our window. Her question made me laugh, which was essential in hard times. She knew just how to pluck my Piscean heart from its depths and give it a light breeze when needed. Now was the time.

Going to the Deep South with my Jewish Middle-Eastern girlfriend sounded exciting and slightly terrifying, but since she was feminine-presenting with blondish hair, I knew it wasn't much of a worry, as messed up as that may sound. My girlfriends before her had been butch, short-haired, and masculine-presenting. That could have been a problem in the South. In fact, an ex-girlfriend, Cassidy, had been beaten up on several occasions for going to the women's restroom while on tour with a popular indie band she roadied for. Some woman would scream to her boyfriend, "There's a guy in here!" and he would burst in to save the day, beat her up, and put her in the hospital with broken ribs or a broken nose. That happened to her multiple times, and it was what Cassidy dealt with being butch and Black, a double whammy that she swallowed deep into her soul until it became crippling pain that created health problems for her.

She wasn't the only butch girlfriend I wished I could protect from this world. My heart was touched by anyone I dated who fell outside the status quo. When I held their hands on the subway, I leant them my freedom, how I looked socially acceptable despite a full head of unruly curls. I was less threatening to society than they were. When I held their hands on the subway, I would imagine I was helping rewrite history, showing the kids on the train that this is what love can look like.

With Noa it was different. She was small and pretty and looked nonthreatening, so when we kissed on the subway or held hands, it was the kind of thing men might store in their minds for later. In the Deep South, I was okay with our relationship sliding under the radar as two "feminine" women who were traveling as friends. The trip to see Mom post-electroshock therapy was stressful enough on its own; I was happy to eschew the added burden of being seen as queer at every backwoods gas station.

But there was something more happening, under the surface. Something in my heart was touched so deeply that someone was coming with me into this moment of life. This dark moment. When the woman I had loved, who had raised me, whom I had counted on, was falling apart. I had gone through her breakdown by proxy, but I hadn't been in the room. I couldn't bear going to see her in the mental hospital. I didn't help her move. I felt awful for that. But I also felt I would have evaporated and fallen through the cracks had I stopped my life to go to her. The enmeshment I was attempting to get out of had the power to grip me tight. And I was barely holding myself up by a thread at the time as I slept on an air mattress at my friend's house, tried to get my film work seen, and attempted to make a living. It was all too precarious to risk leaving it, even for a moment.

But now things were more secure. Noa had moved into my old apartment with me; I had kicked out the subletters because I could afford it again with both of us paying $400 apiece for prime Brooklyn real estate. I pushed her to move in faster than she had wanted, but it was one of those moments when I had to do a hard thing because financially, I couldn't afford it on my own. I had quit my day job of nannying and was making films and writing full-time. But when the time came to go see my mom, when I felt ready, Noa was there in a heartbeat, ready to come with me. At age twenty-nine, I had never felt the warmth of that level of love and support. She was always like that. She was a secure human, and although I'm sure it exhausted her at times, she wasn't scared of my wild emotions and sometimes quiet coldness. Instead, she was patient with me. She loved my fire, my creative passion, my willpower, my discipline, my ambition, and my willingness to play and dance with her at every turn. As my mom, who was the only family I really had, broke down, Noa witnessed me break down. I desperately tried to individuate from the enmeshment with my mother, and it hurt like hell.

Noa and I arrived at JFK too early for our flight, so we ordered a cheese pizza and sat at a terminal spot. Noa pulled a bag of kale out of her backpack and began to rip it into small pieces and put it atop the pizza. That was another reason I loved her. She could do things like that and not bat an eyelash. Of course she brought a bag of kale to the airport, because of course we needed some greens on this voyage into the land of grits and bacon. My heart smiled under the fluorescent lights as the loudspeaker announced flights to Orlando and Houston.

We landed in Alabama, and my mom picked us up in my stepdad's mother's hand-me-down Crown Victoria, which felt like riding in a boat. Her hands shook from the nervousness of seeing me again. We drove through Alabama with the windows down, a warm breeze blowing through and humidity kissing my hair. I drank it all in. I missed the South. The relics of the past lived along highways, dilapidated buildings strangled by bright emerald kudzu and old men seated outside gas stations as if time had forgotten to keep them moving forward. Noa asked questions about everything as an angel of a buffer. She was funny and cute and kept things light, asking things like, "Why do they eat so many biscuits here?" and "Is there a preferred local beer?" My mom loved answering her questions and sharing all the Southern charm and customs with her.

When we got to the vacation trailer community, my mom took us to the trailer that we had rented. On the way in, we stopped at the community hosts, a couple in their seventies, two big bodies plopped into beach chairs upon Astroturf with a sign out front that said "Welcome home!" They asked if Noa and I were sisters. Mom said, "No, just friends." In that moment, I was fine with that; we were good. But later, my mom apologized for answering like that.

"I didn't know what to say. I'm so sorry," she said. I assured her I was fine with it. I didn't need to be the talk of the town while I was there; this trip wasn't about that. My mom told the couple we were from New York City like she was real proud. The woman said that her cousin once went to New York City for a conference and said it was real crowded but that they had the best pizza in the world. I smiled and Noa said, "Oh, yes, the best pizza," in her thick Israeli accent. Their eyes squinted like they couldn't place her, and Mom quickly said bye.

After we settled into our trailer with its twin beds and musty smell of stale cigarettes and mold, we went to see Mom's. As we entered, her hands began to shake again. I noticed her picking up a plastic cup and sipping from it. When she put it down, I slyly peeked inside to see white wine in there. It was only 11 am, but it didn't matter. I understood. This reunion was stressful and awkward. Noa even asked, about five minutes later, "Do you have any white wine?" For her, perhaps it was an Israeli thing. Some white wine on a Saturday morning is okay, nothing to be ashamed of. But for me, I knew there was too much pain in the room, and we couldn't deal, and we all needed a drink. I'm pretty sure Noa felt like she was having an epic experience of the Deep South at a trailer park fantasy, and I'm pretty sure she was fine. But we, my mom and I, were not fine. Not yet. There had been too much pain, too much drama, just too much, between us.

When I was a kid, *glug glug glug* liquid pouring and ice clinking in glasses were a part of the symphony of life. A bold red or a smokey Scotch was perhaps the way the jagged edges of trauma became smoother for my parents. Like rocks by the ocean, the trauma faded, rubbed down to curves from tumbling waves until a new day made them sharp again. Alcohol was a fast fix, and in the '80s and '90s, with full-time work and a kid, stopping to deeply feel and heal was a luxury my parents, working class and hustling, didn't have much space for.

Sweaty after a Sunday round of tennis, a salty ocean sea breeze blowing in with beer on tap with white foam that would leave a mustache, my dad would sit with his friends, getting more and more free and more and more warm, beer by beer. At a certain point, over the music, jangling Cuban pop, he would reveal what was under his drinking: a hot bed of pain from being molested by priests as a kid in the Catholic church and beaten by his father.

"God is a sham! The Catholic church is evil. Those priests abused me! The church is all lies," he'd say as he gulped from his beer glass, slamming it down on the table as some men's faces turned white and others turned away. I became heavy lead as the music jangled louder and louder. I became invisible, too scared to stay in the room. I flew out over my head when my body became still and heavy, and I often didn't return for days. Likely not realizing the impact of his honesty on me, he was clear and stark, aggressive even, about how he had gotten on with life after his horrors and how he would never look back to the church.

For my mom, it was different. I had seen her in therapy for years, taking antidepressants and/or antianxiety meds for a long time, but from what I had deduced, the PTSD of her childhood sexual abuse didn't go away easily either.

I remember once I heard her sobs from the living room, where I sat alone. I had seen her gulp down glasses of red wine, and now smelled the vomit as I approached the bathroom, my knees trembling as the movie *Sliver* played on the TV in the living room with a stalker watching a naked woman from a camera. I was eight. I felt invisible. But she was doing the best she could. She was barely thirty-five and carrying the weight of single parenthood alone—she managed to buy a house, she held down a good job, she got me to Sunday church and ballet and made sure I ate salad.

Back then, I didn't know what a regulated nervous system felt like, or even that it was an option, and I don't blame anyone for that. I knew what fun felt like; my parents were fun! I knew what adventure and culture looked like! I got to travel and learn with them. My mom took me to museums and on history tours of cities and to national parks and plays. My dad took me snorkeling and skiing. But I also craved emotional security and safety, even if I didn't exactly know it.

Perhaps the kids who got those things wished they'd gotten the fun parents who blasted Led Zeppelin and let them stay up late. Perhaps we always want what we don't have.

But just like my parents, I felt my own internal pressure *pop, open, fizz, whoosh,* and release as I sipped my first sweet Malibu rum in the clubs in Brazil at thirteen, and then when I felt the burn of tequila slide down my throat and smelled the smoky Mexican earth kept within that spirit at fourteen. I felt the freedom I had witnessed in my parents after a few drinks.

So, when I noticed mom drinking the white wine to calm her nerves in the trailer that day in Alabama, my first thought was a little judgment and fear, but after that came understanding and a desire to join her. Who was I to judge her for not being able to handle the pain, the anxiety, the collapse of her life? I needed something to smooth the edges of the moment, too. Numbing the pain is so complex. Sometimes it is how we survive. But sometimes it takes away the light in your eyes and you become unrecognizable. If you aren't aware that you are escaping the pain, then you spend life just running and forget why you are running. At some point, the truth always catches up, even if it's just, "I hurt, and this is the only way I know to function." But there is choice there, not unconsciousness. The unconscious numbing and avoidance are scary because the pain gets bigger as it's squashed down; usually our numbing tactics have to get bigger, too, and this can be dangerous. Perhaps for many of our ancestors, that was truly the only way they knew, but for us, there are other ways. There are meetings and groups and therapy and knowledge.

We did our best that day. It was a step in the direction of healing and reunion. Sometimes those moments are messy and you can't do it perfectly. You just do it. And we did.

Later that day, Noa and I swam in the cool blue lake under the raging, scorching southern sun while my mom and stepdad sat on the shore in their beach chairs. Things felt peaceful and soft. We floated and whispered, our bodies close in the water, wrapped together like tangled grass. A hidden dialogue under the surface said things like "This too shall pass" and "All is well." Toes touched mud. Tears mingled with hair stuck to skin. Laughter. Tears. Laughter. Kind words from my mom.

That was the kind of healing you can't pay for. You can't get it in an ayahuasca ceremony or a breathwork session or a spiritual retreat. It's the healing that happens when you stare straight into the pain, and you go there, and you try and keep your heart open. And you don't run. It may be messy. But it is the healing. And soon after, the rebirth.

Moving toward love and connection even when that love and connection has involved pain is scary. You have to stabilize into your body, locate your truth, and stay close to your breath. It takes being rooted and feeling resourced, supported, and strong to be able to open your heart even in the face of pain. This may look like seeing someone who triggers you, or hurt you once, or simply being around family if it's been a complex journey together. Avoiding pain and discomfort won't work. It just won't. We can always take time-outs and breaks, but coming back to the moment, trusting our bodies and beings to be able to show up, despite and amidst pain, and finding love even there, is a great practice. Staying in anger or keeping a closed heart can feel easier, but it often has lasting negative impact on our sweet tender hearts. Sometimes we need years of practicing forgiveness and compassion, releasing anger and grief, before we are able to turn back to places that feel scary to look toward. Finding even a glimmer of love and compassion in our hearts helps us begin to heal and have the courage to feel what is there instead of hiding from or numbing the pain. And it can be a slow process. You won't get every step right. You will numb sometimes or let anger get the best of you, and then you will practice coming back to your heart again. And again. And this will be the practice. With all the hard things. **It takes courage to be with all of it, to not stay closed, to breathe and feel, again and again and again.**

Dare *to* Feel

REFLECTIONS

- In what situations do you tend to turn away from people you love because things got too complicated? What feelings make you want to disengage?

- Have you ever taken a time-out from a challenging situation to allow yourself to heal? How did it feel to reengage?

- In what ways do you tend to numb your feelings instead of feeling them as they arise? What are the consequences and side-effects of using these numbing behaviors?

- Has someone ever come through for you when you needed support to face something tough? What did it feel like to have them help you?

RITUAL FOR PURIFICATION

Sit by a fire and focus your gaze on the flames, or gaze into a candle for a while. Call forth something that feels heated in your heart and see if you can let it dance in the flames. Imagine the energy of the situation going into fire for purification and transmutation. Let it leave your body and let it burn away. Notice the sensations in your body as you engage in this ritual; what does it feel like to allow this thing to move through you? When you feel clear, blow out the candle or douse the flames of the fire, and feel the air element blowing the weight of it all away.

As a bonus, a return to our burning ritual: Write down anything that is weighing on you and burn it in the flames. Phrase it, "I am ready to release X from my mind and my body."

ON HOW TO BE WITH FAMILY

Take note when you are with family:
How many different voices come alive within you?

Give them names and write them down.
For example:

Rejected Sad Little Girl, age 5.
Angsty Pissed Teen, age 15.
Sweet Playful Innocent One, age 3.
Know It All Who Had to Grow Up Too Fast, age 12.
Zany Whacky Ball of Fire, age 8.
Holier than Thou Cold and Aloof, age 25.

Note how each of them sounds
and feels
and how they want to defend,
react,
cry out . . .

Note:
Is one the voice of flight?
Fight?
Freeze?
Is one a cry for help?
The voice of shame?
The voice of hope?

Get to know who is who,
so you don't go thinking
it's ALL the Real You!

Sit and breathe,
and say a reluctant inner
THANK YOU
that your family
has the shamanic magical ability
to call forth the WHOLE
cast of voices and personas
that live within you.

When you depart to return to your own home
and world,
you will know how better to hear those little mad,
and sad,
and wild voices,
to listen to them with love,
to heal them, too.

And then let the
True You
come through.

21

From a Broken Heart
to One That Is Healing

T he light was low. An old lamp from the '70s made half-moon shadows under my father's eyes. Skin sweetly sagged and puffed where once his olive-toned Brazilian skin was smooth. When we traveled together when I was a kid, people used to look at us funny. My skin was alabaster white with freckles and blue cups-of-ocean eyes, and his skin was dark caramel in the summer. More than once, people asked, "Where did you buy her?" as they laughed. He was brown with wiry hair styled in a light afro in the '70's, and I think it pained him that I didn't look more like him. In pictures I see our nose and eye shapes are identical, and 23andMe has confirmed that he is indeed my dad, but back then, in the '80s, a Latin man with leathery skin and a little one with creamy skin was a sight for most.

His apartment in Miami was a mix of furniture from our old home and Rooms To Go specials. In the bathroom were tiny shampoo bottles from the hotels he stayed at as a flight attendant for forty years. They filled up the areas under each sink, and their color had faded from years of not being used, just sitting there in the damp quiet under the sink. He had glasses that said United Airlines in the cupboard and towels that said Sheraton in the bathroom. He was a Brazilian immigrant turned American, and this was his American dream: living on Miami Beach, waking up and seeing the ocean every day. He didn't pine for more, but he relished what he had. That's something he taught me. Once you create your dreams, don't squander them wanting more or thinking about what's next. Take time to celebrate and enjoy.

He was seventy-nine now, and I hadn't been to visit him for a while. I felt guilty about this, but I'd been quietly healing my relationship with him. I didn't want to come back angry. I wanted to come back kind and loving, with forgiveness. When I was eighteen, I said to myself, *I need to forgive him*. I started then, and it took fifteen years.

The AC hummed gently as we sat on the beige leather couches that faced a black and sleeping TV. I had been terrified to visit. In fact, I'd asked several friends if they would come with me for moral support, but no one was able to. The last time I visited him, he and his then wife had grabbed each other in nasty ways in front of me, and she had brought out the worst kind of toxic alpha in him. He commented on my body then, my breasts, told me I was getting overweight, asked me to change outfits or he wouldn't be seen with me because he was embarrassed I wore black. The whole thing was a trauma trigger that I could not swallow. But there I was. Back with him, determined to heal. I was not angry anymore. I was ready. And that was when he said it.

"I'm so sorry your mom and I made your childhood a living hell." The leather couch squeaked and the towel he had laid over it shifted with his weight. That was the way he liked to preserve leather.

I replied, slowly, "I'm sorry, too. I'm sorry I was so angry at you for so many years. I'm so sorry."

Tears dripped from his eyes, and I felt something soft and new in my body. I could not believe that moment was happening. It was a moment I had only dreamed of. He reached out his hand and squeezed mine. My eyes filled with tears.

In the years prior, with the help of breathwork, plant medicine, therapy, and God knows what else, I finally felt forgiveness toward him in my heart. I saw how he and my mom and I were in a perpetual drama triangle, like many families that go through painful divorces, and it was up to me to free myself from the past by saying I was sorry for my anger, coldness, frustration, hardness, and moodiness as a young girl and teen.

I realize most people may not have this conversation with their father, but perhaps I had it for you. I did nearly twenty years of therapy and spiritual practice to get to that moment. I approached that moment alone, terrified I would arrive to mean words and a cold heart. But instead, there was kindness. I had done the internal work for over a decade, and something had shifted within me. I was soft and loving, with no walls up. And out of nowhere, he beat me to the punch. Or perhaps the openness and softness of my heart made an opening for him as well.

Often our daddy issues build up from what we experience as "father," as "man," as "masculine" over the course of a lifetime, personally and collectively, and honestly, we all have to do this healing. Some of us more than others, yes. But we all have a little something to heal with men, Dad, the patriarchy, God . . . It may take a while. For now, for many of us, every lover, every random man at the airport, and every call with Dad is an opportunity to choose healing, or to stay angry or closed. Day to day, it's perhaps a little of both. Forgiveness comes with time and dedication, but it frees a place inside of you where before it all felt like a giant, heavy, tightly clenched iron fist. Forgiveness swoops in, even there, softening those edges. Melting that pain.

If the healing of forgiveness is something you need, imagine you could have that moment with your dad or mom or former best friend or partner. We all know humans we have loved and experienced gut-wrenching pain with, people who have perhaps done things that feel unforgiveable. And we carry that like a granite rock upon our hearts. Over time it becomes heavy. What if you could lay down that burden? What if you could stop holding the pain? There is liberation there, too. It's possible for there to be days when you don't walk around with the heaviness of that weight attached to you.

Sometimes we get more attached to our anger or resentment than the actual thing that caused it, and the idea of being the same person minus the resentment is strange, like shifting an identity. But that is the pain possessing you, and like a demon, it sucks the love and life out of you. Do not get so attached to the pain of the past that you do not allow the possibility of healing to enter. Imagine it is possible. Whether it is with your father, mother, ex-partner, or friend, whether they were awesome or awful, whether they are dead or alive, imagine it, dream it, feel it.

Dare
to
Feel

REFLECTIONS

- What anger or resentments do you still carry when it comes to the heart? Who are they about? How long ago did the things happen that caused the anger and resentment? What was the context?

- What would you need in order to forgive or let go of any of that past anger or resentment?

- Who would you be if you weren't carrying all that baggage anymore? Think deep on this. How would it change you? How would you love without that baggage?

- Do you believe that healing is possible, or are you resigned to the idea that with some situations, there is no way to heal?

- If you could heal your side of the situation, what might that look like?

RITUAL FOR RELEASING RESENTMENT

Create a safe space by your altar, a window, or anyplace that feels good to you, and sit comfortably. Center yourself with a few minutes of deep, intentional breathing, and then bring forth an image of the person who hurt you or caused anger or resentment in you. How does it feel to bring them into your space? Now imagine them as a child who is yearning for love, care, and attention. Then see them as an adolescent, alone and crying in their room. How are your feelings about the resentment starting to shift? Begin to notice any seeds of compassion that start to emerge from your heart. Let it water your release from the bonds of the anger and resentment. Slowly let their image fade from your mind and heart. Take a moment to shake or move your body if you feel a lot there, or to free-write if that would support you to close the ritual.

STRIPPED INTO INFINITE YOU

Who are you without your shame?
Who are you without your guilt?

Love pours through your pores;
you are becoming no one
and everyone.

You are a dancing skeleton
singing with Jerry,
nothing left of your flesh
but tiny rose buds dancing
where nipples once were,
rivers cascading
where eyes once cried,
thunderclaps escaping
where laughter once boomed,
lights flashing
where shadows once loomed.

22

Daring to Let Yourself Feel Loved

I watched the trees blur like Monets as the train sped by and my breath fogged the window. Summer sun poured onto everything, relieving the Pacific Northwest of its usual emo mood. I teetered on the sweet edge of nerves and excitement as I rode a train from Seattle to Portland to see a possible lover, River. He was seven years younger than me, and he made my heart flutter.

We met in a dark room on night one of three ayahuasca ceremonies, his hand on my back as my face met the yellow plastic Tupperware doubling as a puke bucket. He was a leader in that ceremony space and perhaps shouldn't have had the audacity to hit on me, but it was an unorthodox space, and he was an unorthodox guy. The day after all three ceremonies completed, he sat next to me in the bright May light in the Berkley house the group had turned into a mystical, ephemeral temple. He looked at me with gentle, blue eyes and asked, "Can I kiss you?" I giggled and nodded, despite being worried someone would see us. He pressed his lips to mine, and I felt electricity tingle through me.

For over a year after that kiss, we spoke on the phone every week. He was very consistent and was clear he was in a polyamorous relationship. At the time, I wasn't sure about non-monogamy, but I appreciated the love and attention, and our phone calls felt safe. Time had built courage within me and a deep hunger. Call after call, the energy and tension built, and the hunger became bigger than my rational mind. On the train to see him in person, my body fizzed and grew breathless.

This was a leap as so much time had passed since we were together in the flesh. What if I was chasing a fantasy? What if the chemistry had gone? I traced my finger on my lip and turned the volume up as James Blake's album *Overgrown* blasted through my headphones.

River picked me up from a friend's house on the Fourth of July, and I had the audacity to wear a red cotton knit dress and black heels, both completely inappropriate for these festivities in Portland. I often forgot that I no longer lived in New York, where dressing up for any occasion is fine, even expected. In the Pacific Northwest, however, July 4th means maybe some flat sandals, loose sundresses, T-shirts, and jeans. I was committed to my aesthetic, though in retrospect I blush, feeling like it was way too on the nose for me to arrive in a hot red dress and heels. But I suppose I had worked hard to rid myself of the shame I often felt around my desire to free my sensual being and allow myself to be "too much." So, there I was at 4 pm in Portland, looking like a sex goddess femme fatale.

As he pulled into the driveway, I fidgeted and picked at the skin around my cuticles, the telltale betrayal of how I really felt, a bad habit I had picked up from my mom as a kid. I did not know I was about to have two of the most special days, but I was ready for an evening of fun—yet I was also unsure whether I would be attracted to him anymore. As I opened the car door of his beat-up Infiniti, I smiled. His presence calmed me, and his blue eyes reached inside me and tickled my insides. His smile was bright.

"Roxo! Welcome to Portland!"

I sank into the bucket seat and laughed hearing him address me by my last name.

Later that evening, we sat down for dinner outside his dad's home, which was empty and up for sale. He lived in the apartment above the garage, but we cooked dinner in the big open kitchen, which echoed with our voices. The space was naked except for the memories that hung in the air, which River alluded to every now and then.

He pulled out a free local newspaper, balancing his elbows on the wooden table out back as the sky filled with dusk colors overhead, and began to read my horoscope.

"Pisces, you have strong intuitive skills this week. Use them wisely. Open your heart to the man sitting in front of you. He is very sexy and excited to see you . . ."

Maybe it was cheesy, but it stole my heart and made me giggle like a teenager, my stomach full of butterflies leaving their cocoons. In fact, I was a butterfly leaving her cocoon.

After dinner, with great confidence, he led me up into his apartment, which was lit by candles. He must have done it while I was in the bathroom. Wow. I laughed to myself at his moves. He was truly pulling out all the stops, and I loved every bit of it. He brought me up to his lofted bed and didn't miss a step. I giggled with nervousness, even though he was younger than me and I thought I must be more experienced. Right? He was the embodiment of Lover, seducing me in a way that I desperately wanted to be seduced. His apartment smelled like palo santo and looked like the room of a spiritual dude—books on alchemy and tinctures; rapé tobacco snuff in little jars; an altar with an image of Shiva, though to me he was Krishna, a lover of women and a lover of love. Without words, he laid me on the bed and began to undress me with so much love and confidence, and a splash of mischief.

There is a way a man looks at a woman, like she is the most divine gift on earth. It is a look of admiration, of utter pleasure and joy. It is a look that is also a bow. It says, "I see you. Goddess. Woman. Divine treasure. I honor you." It is a fulfillment of birth to be seen like that by anyone. A man gazing upon the divine feminine incarnate, naked round flesh shining like gold and diamonds, soft pink petals below, hardening sweet nipples, and eyes glistening, overflowing with soul. I hope every woman is gazed upon in that way by whomever she desires at least once in her lifetime.

He wooed my body slowly that night, being careful not to rush. He was confident and dominant in a way that made me melt to my core. As I laid naked in the bed, he left the room for a moment and came back holding a spoon. I stuck my head between the railings of the lofted bed and he fed me coconut ice cream. I was a baby bird, my mouth open, sucking down delicious, soft, white love upon love upon love.

He took me to the local bathhouse the next day, and as we sat in the steam room, he looked at me and asked, "First time here, ma'am?"

And in a southern accent, I said, "Why yes, it is. I am new in town. Just arrived from Kansas, searching for a new life . . ." And we played back and forth until he grabbed me and kissed me and fed me Honey Mama's chocolate for the first time with my head in his lap. The staff at the bathhouse had to come tell us that we weren't allowed to touch since everyone was naked. But our bodies couldn't abide by such a rule; they were magnets, and they were living their own story, perhaps lifetimes in the making.

After two days of kissing, crying, laughing, cooking, and dancing together, we sat during magic hour under a cotton-candy pink sky, and my whole being melted like butter.

River looked at me and said, "I'm going to draw us a bath." He walked upstairs in the empty house, his footsteps echoing through each room, and I could hear him turn the water on. My heart flooded with "It's almost time to leave" pain and "I can't believe I can feel this good" love.

He came back downstairs and gently took my hand and led me up the wooden stairs. The tiny bathroom was filled with candles, and the claw-foot tub slowly filled with water. The room smelled like roses yet there were none visible. The full-bodied rose scent from essential oil and rose water merged with the bath water and wafted up to meet me. We were both silent. It was one of those moments when you enter into the sacred domain, when you get chills up your spine, when you don't have to say what's happening because it just feels magical. Those moments are often unplanned. They are strokes of grace when you and another feel the divine moving through and you know not to disturb it by talking.

We both took our clothes off and entered the water, one of us at each end of the tub, as the dim glow of the candles and the steam rising from the water made everything feel surreal.

"I want to sing to you," he said. "Close your eyes."

I wish I could remember what he sang, but I just remember the feeling in my chest, where all doubts that I was unlovable rushed out the door in a fury and a feeling of pure unconditional love moved in. I felt tears stream down my cheeks onto my bare chest and mingle with the waters like little diamond prayers.

I had never felt more loved than I did in that moment. It was like I needed to spend the two prior days melting all my walls so I could truly feel that gift. I had to open so much to receive it. Life had offered me moments like that before, but I wasn't available for them; now I was. Fully. Nothing in me said no to love or unconsciously pushed it away.

Tears streamed into the water, and the moment was etched in time. Though I knew he probably wasn't my life partner, the gift he gave me was a reminder that I was worthy of a deep and divine love. The days I spent with him raised the bar for me, and I felt confident to embrace my desire to be fully met by an equal in the sacred realms of loving.

Sometimes the heart work comes in beautiful, magical ways. "The work" is not always hard. It's not always heavy. It can be joyful and playful and fun to risk opening the heart and feeling something new, or believing in love again and feeling excitement at the risk of trusting someone new. Healing the heart after heartbreak can be fun, sweet, tender, and simple. It may be teasing and laughing and kissing that is a balm on the old wounds. We don't always have to cry alone on our meditation cushions. **Sometimes we have to heal in connection. And it can be such a pleasure to do so.**

Dare to Feel

REFLECTIONS

- When has your own healing journey surprised you? When has healing come in a gentle way, a way that felt fun and exciting and not like heavy labor?

- When and what have you healed through pleasure and joy? Consider the moments when pleasure healed something in you, and when joy healed something in you.

- When has intimate connection been the best balm for your heart? What did it feel like to open to intimacy even when you felt scared? Even when you weren't sure what would come of it?

- When have you felt undoubtedly loveable? Name the moments when you felt utterly loved and cared for and completely seen. Write them out in detail.

- When considering your soul's journey, what soul lessons are connected to love for you?

RITUAL FOR SELF-LOVE

Set your ritual space in the bathroom and create your own rose ritual bath. Light some candles and turn the overhead lights off. (If you have pink salt lamps, even better.) Put rose petals and/or rose oil in the tub as it fills. Let the steam from the hot bathwater fog the space. Play some soft music that feels sensual and gentle to you. Take a moment to gaze at yourself in the mirror in the warm, low light. As you enter the bath, whisper the things you consider lovable about you to yourself. For example, "You are so precious, my love," or "You are a beacon of divine love on this planet." As you soak, sing a song to yourself, as if you are your own divine lover serenading your soul. Then sing to your future beloved, to the gods and goddesses, to the trees . . . to whomever and whatever lights up your heart. Save the rose petals in a bowl by your altar for when you need to remember this bath of love.

TO BE LOVED

When you find yourself being loved unconditionally,

say THANK YOU to the heavens!

Praise the miracle that it is!

Teach your nervous system in that moment

this is what love feels like.

Love that is unconditional.

Love that doesn't judge me for my fucked-up-ness.

This is real love.

Love that just loves.

23

Meeting Heart Shadows
with Love

Even after we commit to living from the heart, open and feeling it all, we will still have moments of deep rupture, and moments when we have to confront our shadows. Only now, we have more resources and courage and skill to meet these parts with love and have patience as they transform. We will always have feelings that come from a part of us that is in pain, stuck in the past, stuck in trauma, still mad, sad, angry, annoyed at Mom/Dad/God, etc. Everyone has these places inside. No one is immune. Yet as you connect more with the feeling world inside of you, you can begin to distinguish where a feeling may be coming from. You identify less with passing moods or parts, and you learn to look at them with a discerning and compassionate gaze. You look at them with love.

For instance, I have this very fatalistic part inside of me that says things like, "See, I knew they wouldn't come through and I would have to do it myself. It's fine. I am the only person I can count on." That story comes with a feeling of disappointment. It feels like a heavy cloak on my body. It slows me down. It steals my joy and life force. And it's only in the last few years that I've been able to feel it exactly when it shows up and identify that it is not "me" but an old defense mechanism that came to prevent me from being hurt. "If I decide I am alone or not fulfilled by something first, then I don't have to bear the discomfort of being disappointed or abandoned or rejected."

ny patterns. We could call her Existential Emo Eliza.
nough that when each little bit of disappointment
, I don't trust I need to always go there. I know there
I need to grieve (like when my mom was sick in the
hospital), but when I anticipate sadness and disappointment—saying
things like, "They are probably going to leave anyway, I may as well
go"—I know this is a voice and a feeling born from my wounding, and
I know better than to let it run the show.

I encourage everyone I work with to get to know the voices inside
and label them according to their story. Study them so you know who
is speaking to you and when. Many people either open the floodgates
to feel all the things coming through or they choose to feel nothing at
all because the art of discernment when it comes to feeling is harder. It
requires actual internal awareness skills. Emotional jedi skills.

Below are a few of my favorite archetypal patterns born from wounds
or trauma that I see in people in workshops, media, and culture at large.
Keep a pen handy and notice if any of these are ones you embody on
the regular. But first, don't judge yourself. Try and approach each one
with equanimity. Likely you created that pattern, a brilliant persona, to
protect yourself and keep your truth safe. So, just because you notice a
pattern doesn't mean you need to kill it off. Perhaps it's time to let it off
duty and give it a new job, but with loving kindness.

We all have a chorus of shadow selves waiting to take the inner
stage at any moment. They line up and say: "Is it time for my close-up?"
They press powder to their cheeks. They arrive in costume; they are
ready to jump at the sound of a snap. They rise and possess you before
you have even noticed! Notice if you recognize any of the shadow
selves listed below from your own inner world, and also what emotion
they are hiding. Underneath them all is Love, is a broken heart, a fear
of trust, a desire to be held, a fear of vulnerability . . . Underneath
them all is the possibility for healing and change. Feel free to under-
line the ones you see or feel most often within yourself and note what
emotion is under each.

Dare
to
Feel

REFLECTIONS

Circle your top five shadow selves from the list below. Ask yourself what emotion each of those shadow selves is hiding. What desire is this emotion connected to? (For example, if you circle the Victim, you might notice that the emotion hiding under it is shame, which comes from a desire to be respected.)

SHADOW SELVES

- The Victim ready to moan, "Woe is me!"
- The Martyr ready to say, "I'm fine; don't worry about me."
- The Cold Bitch icing us with her glacial stare.
- The Asshole ready to say, "Fuck you!"
- The Savior ready to hop in and save us all.
- The Grump ready with a negative retort.
- The Brat with her scowl and stomping feet.
- The People Pleaser ready to say yes to anything.
- The Nervous Nelly fidgeting and worried.
- The Hyper Vigilant checking all the doors and tracking everyone's moves.
- The Control Freak constantly saying, "That's not how to do it!"

- The Judge Judy analyzing what is right and wrong.
- The Lazy Lu ready to disengage and binge on trash TV.
- The Avoidant who keeps busy to avoid deep feeling and/or conflict.
- The Emo who oozes sadness and existential pain.
- The Sentimental Syrup who bleeds her honey heart all over to try and pull you in.
- The Spacey Ditz who says, "Haha, I don't know!" to avoid what she does know.
- The Suspicious One who never trusts anyone and never opens up.
- The Fake who says, "I love your dress!" with a high-pitched, insincere tone.
- The Know-It-All who one-ups everyone and never has to be vulnerable.
- The Too-Cool-for-School One who acts like they don't give a fuck to cover up that they do.

Feel free to create your own shadow self and add it to this list! There are infinite options.

RITUAL FOR SHADOW EMBODIMENT

Set your ritual space. Pick one of your top five shadow selves from the list above and choose a theme song for it. Play the song, let yourself get a bit weird, and try to embody this self FULLY. Try it on, dance, feel it, maybe stomping your feet as your bratty shadow, or getting super emo or suspicious. Do this once without seeing yourself, and then a second time while watching yourself in the mirror. Go all the way! How does it feel in your body to embody this shadow self? This will begin to plant the seeds of transformation so that next time the pattern arises, you recognize it more quickly and can choose something different.

YOUR WOUNDS ARE GOLD

*You have been given a brilliant tool for awakening in this life . . .
it is that thing you dislike most about yourself!*

*That habit, that pattern,
the one you wish you could erase!*

*This is your key
to the Real You.*

*The awakened you,
the peaceful you!*

The happy you!

The realized you!

*But if you hide away from that thing,
if you try and lock it in a closet,
ignoring it,
avoiding it,
ashamed
and embarrassed . . .
you may miss out
on becoming whole!*

*It may take years
to take that thing,
that habit,
that pattern
and FREE IT
so you can transform it!*

And this process,
this whole caboodle,
is how you make art
out of your life!

This painful,
elaborate,
alchemical
process
is
how
you
turn
shit
into
gold.

Opening the Heart to
Receive Big Love

I looked at the rows of shoes, winter clothes spilling out of a duffle bag stuffed fat and tucked under the hems of hanging dresses, the blue carpet nearly exfoliating my face with its tiny synthetic edges as I lay cheek down, artificial light spilling bright and warm onto my tear-streaked face. I took a big breath as I wrapped my arms tightly around myself, clenching my whole body as small as it would go into a ball of tense sadness.

I was thirty-seven and still needed a private place for a deep cry. And you know what, I was perfectly okay with that. My heart was free to feel now, without shame. My heart was open after years and years of healing, and I knew this didn't mean there wouldn't be hard days. It was my practice now to feel, to stay open, and to not ignore my heart. This was conscious relating. There were no masks of acting cool here. No avoiding. This was a practice of staying with the heart, even when it still hurt.

When my partner and I had a rupture, I needed a place to sob freely. I didn't want to hurt him with my sobs; I didn't want my sobs to beg for his love. I didn't want him to feel bad for me and come comfort me out of pity. I wanted to sob freely and privately in the only space that seemed the most soundproof, the gentlest, the most like a tomb or cocoon. There I lay, among colorful fashion and soft fabrics that caressed me. I could let go there and not feel like I was an inconvenience or a victim. I could cease to be strong. I could melt into the carpet. I could be alone.

As much as I wanted to be alone, I was learning that it was not always fair to ask for that within a deep connection with another. When one heart is pulled (often quickly and violently) out of connection, the other person is impacted. The pain we cause when we rip our hearts away is an invisible aggression. We can softly say, "I just need to be alone." And yes, of course, we have every right to do so. But a heart pulled out of a loving bond too quickly causes damage. Trust is broken there. If the bond is old and deep and anchored in roots that reach way under the topsoil, it will likely withstand the force. But when a bond is newer and someone retracts the heart without explanation, that effect can be long-lasting. Trust can be broken. Because that bond has taken time to form through sweet texts, afternoon hangouts, walks, and laughs, the roots are just starting, and the bond needs care.

In our early years, as I worked hard to receive his love, my Beloved always came when he could to fetch me out of the swamp I fell into when I had lost touch with my heart. **It is a pact within a sacred partnership: "If you lose the way home, I will come for you. If I lose my way, you will come for me. If we are both lost, someone must find a way to outstretch a hand and come back to the heart."** And this last piece is where the practice really is, where the ego must die, where someone must reach a hand out first through the deepest pains, stories, and "rights" and "wrongs." Someone must accept the crucible of going first, of putting one's ego down on behalf of the bond. This was one of the most beautiful and surprising things about entering conscious and sacred partnership. This was an uplevel into relating in the deep, vulnerable way I had craved my whole life, but I had much work to do before I was ready for it.

Within the trusting container of sacred partnership, in the phase of deep opening, soul to soul, when I was lost, far from the heart, sinking into a slimy swamp with mud sucking on my toes and dark waters lapping at my ankles, I began to fade away. And I will admit, I could not always reach my hand out to come back to the bond, though I knew doing so was my duty. Sobs that started as cathartic could quickly become a slide into the deep, a visit to the bottom of my pain. But when my partner was able, he came to make sure I stayed on solid ground, to see that I didn't drown within the swamp and spend days walking around like a sad zombie with leeches sucking at my blood and thick, poisonous water moccasins wrapping their tongues around my legs, ready to pounce on whoever came close.

He reminded me who I truly was in those moments. His eyes were a light within a world that was turning dark around me as voices in my mind flared up, protectors inside me showed up with battle cries, and everything in me said, "GIVE UP! RUN!"

What felt most important in such a moment of opening to big, beautiful love was learning to stop identifying with every voice I heard within, especially when the voice arose in moments of conflict and upset. ESPECIALLY then. Learning to discern and pick apart the voices, to be a detective and wonder what they are protecting us from feeling, what they are scared of—this was and is the work. If we simply listen to them without discernment, they will keep us where we are. This is why we get stuck. We want love but can't receive it. We want success, but we are blocking it. It is so simple, yet so complex.

The journey of opening to love can feel as confronting as the journey of meeting your deepest shadows or healing the most ingrained patterns. People may make receiving love look simple. But for some of us, it is not. It requires being the most vulnerable you have ever been. Letting someone in deeper than ever. Giving up control. Trusting that this time it will be different, even if there is no data to prove it. Noticing when fear tries to keep you closed instead of open to love. It is a major threshold to cross: to receive deep, present, conscious love. It separates the lustful, immature, whimsical loves born from wounds and shadow from a deep love born from conscious choice. It can be disarming and disorienting. It may make all your patterns arise, yet again. But this time you have clarity and can see them. They aren't hijacking your life. You are committed to love now. **The practice is to remember who we are, who we really are, which underneath all of it is love.**

Dare
to
Feel

REFLECTIONS

- How do you pull your heart away from intimacy when it feels too scary? Do you go quiet? Numb? Get fiery? Do you get bitchy? Cold? What are your own heart's defenses? (Yes, this is one we keep returning to because it's a big one!)

- When and where do you allow yourself space to fully melt into emotion? In the tub? While working out? Practicing breathwork? How often does this happen?

- What behaviors do you notice creeping in when you feel your heart close down, numb, or harden? What does that feel like in your body?

- Can you accept that the transformational path of the heart means you cannot escape hurt? What does that bring up for you? What would keep you devoted to the path even though it hurts sometimes?

- What inspires you to stay open and risk hurt again and again and again?

RITUAL FOR CLARITY ON WHAT
THE HEART NEEDS

Set your ritual space. Create a cheat sheet for a loved one on what to do when you pull your heart away. It could be making you laugh, or saying, "I see you and I'm not going anywhere." It could be simply bringing you a cup of tea with no words. It could include reminders, like, "Touch is too much for me when I am closed and upset. But kind words are welcome." Spend some time with this. When you're finished, present your cheat sheet to them with love, saying, "Thank you for caring for my heart."

THE PATH OF FIRE

The path of fire means not being attached to outcomes.
It means throwing oneself into the flames for
total transmutation again and again!
It is the accelerated path.
The "I don't fuck around" route.
The Waze app route to "I came here to expand!"

This doesn't mean it's not fun
or that it's not magical as fuck!

But the path of fire is not the run-of-the-mill,
vanilla,
or the "chill" path.

It is not superficial,
and it is not a surface path.

It is that path that's as deep as the oceans
and as high as the mountains.

And you,
you know what I'm talking about, don't you?

You know what it feels like to rise.

You know what it feels like to burn.

You know what it feels like to be reborn.

That's what you came to Earth to do.

You don't try and run when shit gets real.

Even when you're in the face of the scariest of scary, you open.

Because the path of fire is the path of the HEART.

That sacred burning heart that burns away the dark
and yearns to open again and again and again,
and surrender to the full force of LOVE.

25

The Heart That Dares to Ask for Help

I stepped into the center of the circle. There were thirteen women, a perfect number, like the number of moons in a year, like the number of women in a coven. It was late summer, and I had chosen to wear a baby blue silk dress with princess sleeves that felt both beautiful and safe. I was nervous, moving to a new place, out of a big city and into a mountain town. I literally felt like a Pisces fish out of water, far from the things I knew: the bustle of New York and LA, the culture, the grit, the humidity, the traffic, the fashion, the intensity. I moved to Boulder, Colorado, because I fell in love with a man who loved the mountains, the pristine air, the quiet, and the beauty of nature. And I had moved all my things there, my whole heart, and soul, and life.

One week after arriving at the sublet we rented as we searched for a forever home, I found out I was pregnant. Ten weeks later, I found out the pregnancy didn't progress. It was my first three months in a new town, away from all my friends and family, in the high altitude and dry summer of Colorado. Now I was waiting for my body to bleed naturally, to miscarry. I was praying for a miscarriage that simply . . . happened, where my body caught up to the fact that the embryo didn't form and it simply let go. But I was a mess. Hormonally. Psychologically. We were living in my partner's friend's garage apartment as we searched for a home, sharing one room, and I felt immense grief and vulnerability, loss and fear.

But somehow, despite the feelings of emotionally nudity, I said yes to coming to the women's circle. I was desperate for support and beyond trying to keep calm and carry on. All my friends were far away, and FaceTime was simply not cutting it. That night my partner went out with his friends to a concert, and I needed space from him. There are things that women's bodies experience that men will never understand. Maybe intellectually he understood that my body and soul were in a process of letting go, a metaphorical death, but he couldn't feel what it was like to be in my body as it changed drastically, to have felt new life blossoming, to feel the hormones raging and shifting, the constipation that had me screaming, the grief I was now feeling. I needed to be with women. My body needed to be with women.

Zahara, who had called this circle together, dropped us in and created the space. There was sweet smoke, song, directions called in, and silence.

Then she asked, "Who has something to release?"

I stepped into the center of the circle of women I didn't know and told them, "I have been pregnant for ten weeks, but I found out Monday that the pregnancy didn't progress. And now I am waiting to miscarry . . ." My voice broke into sobs. That was me feeling, in front of strangers, and it was hard. But it was what I needed to do. It was my grieving process.

I told them I was trying to ask my body to let go naturally so I didn't have to get a D&C. Though that procedure has saved millions from unwanted pregnancy, in that moment, the last thing I wanted was to go through an abortion. I wanted my body to catch up to the fact we were no longer pregnant, to let go.

Several women came into the circle and began to hold parts of my body. One blonde, beautiful, willowy Dutch woman cradled my head. Another woman placed her hands on my feet. I sobbed and wailed in the center of the circle, and Zahara shouted, "Anyone who is bleeding, press your womb against hers!" Two women came and sandwiched me between them, pressing their bellies and wombs against mine. I sobbed and sobbed. Someone stroked my head.

I didn't think I could open up like that to strangers in this very moment, but I did. Because I was at the edge. I could have stayed home alone, "home" being a one-room sublet apartment with a half kitchen in my partner's friend's garage. I could have stayed there, watched TV, checked out, and cried alone. It took so much courage to say yes to coming to this circle while my whole world felt like it was falling apart.

Just months prior I had guest-taught on a Netflix show in the Caribbean. I had been living my life in Venice, LA, seeing friends, going to Pilates, having clients come to my home, recording podcasts, and taking weekend drives along the Pacific Coast Highway. I was invited to the best parties on the wellness scene. Now I was here in Colorado without a home, far from friends and amidst deep grief. Everything that would usually provide me safety and comfort was gone. I had to show up to feeling it all; there was really no other option.

The women in the circle wiped my tears. They spoke to me and said, "Your time to be a mother will come soon!" and "I feel the spirit of your baby in the room. It's just not time yet." Some sung over my womb, and eventually I found a smile, a softening, and even some laughter. I said, "Okay, you've given me way more attention than I've had in a while. I feel loved and full, so let me give someone else the stage now." I had a strong practical side that could show up even in the most dark or painful moments with humor and love. THANK GODDESS! I thanked the women for holding my heart, grief, and pain and wiping my tears.

That night, I felt safer and more loved than I had felt in a very long time, simply because I chose vulnerability. I chose risk. I chose feeling. I chose opening. I chose emotional nudity. Transparency. Honesty.

A week later, I sat with a few of those same women by the creek, eating grapes, and I felt a stirring in my womb, some light cramping like maybe my period was starting. And it was. That night, my partner happened to be off-grid camping with his nephew, and that was the night I miscarried. It was no regular period; it was twelve hours of laboring alone. It was the most intense pain I had ever experienced in my life. And there was nothing to do except feel it. It never occurred to me that I could go to the ER and ask for pain medicine. The only thought in my mind was that I was doing it; my body was releasing, and I was capable of feeling the pain.

I moved from the shower to the toilet and back and forth all night, writhing in pain and listening to one song on repeat on my phone: a mantra for compassion, Tara's mantra sung by Buddhist monks. Eventually the pain stopped, and I felt relieved. I went to Whole Foods to buy pads and granola. I was exhausted and famished. I went back to our sublet where the gardeners were just arriving for their work. And then I fell to the ground. Something happened. Something was happening. I made it to the bathroom and vomited. The pain was excruciating. It made the pain of the night before seem small. I couldn't even scream. I could barely breathe.

These were the contractions. Whatever happened last night was the labor prior. I had been alone for twelve hours, and I was once again going through it alone, terrified. What ensued was the deepest pain I have ever felt. Somehow, between contractions, I had it in me to text and ask for help. I texted the women I knew in Boulder. I texted my friends in New York, LA, and Seattle. All on one text, I asked for prayers. I felt silly doing it, but as I laid on the bathroom floor next to blood and vomit, alone, that was my only thought. Vulnerability seemed scary. Asking strangers for help was terrifying. Even disrupting my friends' days felt stupid in moments.

I was the same little girl, now in a woman's body, who had done so much on her own, who always had trouble asking for help, who could always power through. Do it on her own. Without anyone. Only child. Working mother. Father far away. She could hold her own pain. I had linked myself into that identity so much that in that moment, I felt ashamed to ask for help. I felt like I should be strong enough to face it on my own, but I sent the group text anyway.

Soon after I sent the text, messages flooded in. My best friends in New York and LA asked if any of the women in Boulder could come support me. Two of my partner's friends said they would come help. My heart was smashed into a million pieces. Yet again, my courage to ask for help was met with love. How couldn't it be? But how often do we not ask for what we need for fear of rejection or because we feel shame?

The contractions came back for another hour or so, and then they stopped. I laid like a torn rag doll on the bathroom floor. There was lots of blood, but it was done. Two amazing women, Martha and Meg, brought me juice, herbs, and Advil, and Meg helped me come back into my body with words, touch, and love. I could barely move from the exhaustion. Soon after, my partner returned home and held me and cared for me deeply.

Later, I found out from my naturopath that I had experienced labor without the good brain cocktail of hormones that helps with the pain. I'd had to face it fully sober.

I bled for a month or so after, until one day, as I was crouching to sit on a meditation cushion, a ball of goo the size of a plump fig slid out of me. My partner and I buried all the tissue I saved in our garden and said prayers and cried again over it. That was my first month in Boulder. A vulnerable asking for help. A radically honest time. There was no looking cool, no holding it together, no feeling fancy or special. There was simply feeling and asking for help.

Sometimes we are pushed to an edge where we have no other choice but to ask for help, to go out on a limb, to risk being rejected or looking silly. It's in these moments when our hearts transform. Walls we have built that keep us "safe" begin to crumble. We start to melt the things that keep us separate and we move into deeper connection. It is very vulnerable in these moments to surrender and stop trying to hold it all together and simply ask for help, or let yourself be seen. But when we are at an edge of loss or grief, we are too tired to fight, too tired to maintain appearances and hold it all together. This is when our greatest transformations happen. We can choose to stay "safe" and protected, or to look someone in the eye and share our pain, our truth. And most likely, our pain or truth will call forth theirs, and connection will be made. Most likely our ask for help will crack open other hearts who want to love and step forward. Most likely our honesty will be a shattering of falsities in any room. **It takes courage**

to reveal our honest grieving or ravaged heart, to reach out a hand and ask for help, to live vulnerably, but that vulnerable place is the perfect match for love to find us, for support and connection to come in. It can feel risky, but it is worth it.

Dare
to
Feel

REFLECTIONS

- When have you dared to ask for help even though you didn't want to? What feelings are present now when you think about asking for help?

- When have you brought your pain or grief into your community, even though it would have been easier to face it alone? If doing this is hard for you, why is this?

- How can you practice surrendering your need to be self-sufficient and trusting the people in your life?

- In what situations do you let yourself be deeply held, and what would it feel like to extend this to other areas of your life?

RITUAL FOR ASKING FOR SUPPORT

Practice asking for help for a week. When you are having a tough time, ask someone you love for support, and be specific about the sort of help you would like. Ask to be held or hugged without words or advice. Ask for them to support you by picking up dinner on the way over to your house. Ask for them to accompany you on an appointment or to hold your hand. Ask for them to look after your child while you take a bath. Ask for an introduction that could help you in your career. What feelings come up for you as you contemplate engaging in this ritual? Where do these feelings come from? Notice if you can ask for help and then accept what is offered without managing or changing it, but simply receiving it as is.

HOW IT FEELS WHEN YOU OPEN

A billion orgasms,
the shock of lightning parting the black sky,
the rage of rivers bursting free from manmade dams
like Berserkers running into battle in a state of ecstatic, blissful rage.

That is the force of a woman opening to her depths.

My knees shake,
I feel the grandmothers hold me.

I look to my sides and see my sisters opening,
releasing . . .

We nod when we know the room is open,
alive in full ceremony;
the healing can happen now.

We shoot sharp glances across when we are afraid
and need each other to come quick
as we usher out the imprisoned pains
and woes
and grief
and tears,
the holding back
and the being stuck,
the fears and fears and fears!

We send those thoughts and experiences,
pains and woes
to the heavens

and into the earth
as sobs,
sighs,
moans,
heaves,
stories.

And a light befalls the room,
a density lifts.

This is where we find freedom.

26

Compassion: Risking for Love

One day on our travels through India, we spent an afternoon at a monastery in Kathmandu witnessing a beautiful ritual with young monks dancing in colorful costumes complete with the sounds of a drum and conch shell, and with so much pomp and circumstance our jaws dropped. An ageless Buddhist nun and teacher from the monastery, Belinda, walked with us into town. It was still light out, but the sky was hazy blue, a color common under the smog of Kathmandu. The monastery was up on a hill, overlooking the town, so we began the downward walk together.

Belinda was British, smart-talking, and worldly, and her words always fell like an arrow in my heart, piercing some part of me that needed to be touched. She said things, like "Well, you all incarnated into one of the countries with the worst karma on this planet. So that karma is yours. You are it. You are not separate from it." And I felt the truth in her words as I felt the history of America, the stolen lands and genocide of many tribes, the unhealed unrepaired wounds with the Indigenous humans, the slavery and stolen children and women and murders of so many, the colonization and invasion of so many countries on behalf of capitalism. The list of America's karmic tragedies goes on and on. And Belinda reminded us, "You are in the heart of it because you are needed there. And this is your karma to behold."

Belinda led the way for us down the hill. As we swung around a corner, voices loud and cheerful, our laughter bouncing off buildings, we saw a man lying in the street. Belinda went silent, and we all followed her hush. She went over to the man and spoke to him in Nepali: "Are you okay? Can you hear me?" The man was out of it; he could barely sit up, and he couldn't really speak but a blur of words. As Belinda attempted to communicate with him, locals started coming out of the homes and shops that surrounded us. There we were, a bunch of New Yorkers and a British Buddhist nun on a hill outside Kathmandu, and it was a sight to see for anyone who wished. Belinda went over to a shop owner outside a tiny grocery and asked for water for the man, perhaps some soup. The woman said something to Belinda to the effect of, "He is always like this," and Belinda responded, "It doesn't matter. We will still care for him as a community." Sah went over and bought the water and soup, and the rest of us stood there, not knowing what to do, perhaps a bit scared or shocked but also not wanting to swoop in and hover. Belinda was in control, and we were simply present.

She sat beside the man and lifted water to his lips, but he was so far gone he could not drink. She looked at us and said, "If someone you loved was hurting, regardless of whether what they did was stupid, wouldn't you help them? Wouldn't you see them as your mother or brother and love them? This is the path. It is not simply meditating. It is stopping and looking beyond the self and caring for each other."

We were all silent, knowing we had walked by so many suffering beings in New York City or Los Angeles as we clicked away on our phones on the way to fabulous parties or client sessions or Pilates classes or beach days. There was a truth in her words. How do we care for each other? How do we dare to feel the pain of the person on the street and stop?

As we all quietly watched, Belinda left the food and water with him; then we continued walking down the hill. Our laughter was hushed now. Our energies were calmed. Something inside of all of us was touched. Belinda had not skipped a beat; there was nothing in her that even questioned stopping and helping this man. Her life was devoted to helping others. She saw every being as an extension of herself; her heart was trained to be compassionate. Those hours of meditation and service were not simply for her; they were for this deep training.

How could we all keep calm and carry on if we stopped to feel the truth of living in this capitalist, self-oriented, success-driven world? If we stopped to feel how many humans around the world are hungry, how many animals are displaced without forest homes, could we keep filling the Amazon cart and getting mani-pedis? If we stopped to feel, could we notice the things that are off and start the process of repair in our neighborhoods, towns, and cities? Could we look at a map of the places we have impacted as a nation, divvy them up, and begin to raise money to create support systems for them?

My friend Shannon and I have been friends for nearly twenty years. Shannon pours a lot of her heart into her neighborhood and into social justice. She created a biweekly potluck in her area that consistently brings together white, brown, and unhoused folks, old and new residents, and many who have been displaced from the neighborhood they grew up in. The first gatherings were interesting. White folks arrived with neatly covered casseroles, and the unhoused folks who live in the park were hanging out, imbibing their preferred substance, while the folks who spend their days in the park chatting and playing cards were just doing their thing. Young folks and children showed up, too. It was a hodgepodge of life stories and lifestyles intersecting each other, melding worlds of difference over food and laughter. Shannon created ways for the different folks to engage with each other. She introduced one to another, and a bridge was formed. This is the kind of thing Shannon does.

She also gathers with other organizers and champions causes. She applies for grants that would beautify and support her neighborhood, helps local artists get their work on murals, and has made friends with everyone in a five-block radius of her home. This is Shannon doing her part to repair the damage of her ancestors, to try and create the world she wants to live in. She lives for more than just herself. She always has.

Though she doesn't have thousands of followers online and she doesn't make millions, Shannon is one of the most inspiring people I know.

What if, instead of (or in addition to) spending thousands of dollars on the self, we each gave a little back to this world, trusting generosity to heal us? What if we each went out on a limb and risked failure by attempting to bring our love into our neighborhood, our building, our community? And what if doing that made us feel whole? Cooking for people, visiting elderly that have no families, planting things where there is no greenery. What if that was what ultimately healed us and brought us together again?

Daring to feel creates a compassionate heart. When we feel the suffering of the wider world, we cannot help but to create empathy and compassion. Feeling beyond our own body and story and into the world around us connects us to it. Of course, the shadow of that is the feeler who feels everything everywhere and gives too much and needs healthy breaks and boundaries, but there are more feelers of the opposite nature out there in this world: those who cannot feel beyond the self and therefore do not stop to support others or extend compassion. When the mind is busy and focused on the self, we walk past people who need us; we miss a comment from a loved one needing support. Feeling our hearts extend into each room we are in connects us to the whole. We can feel other cultures, we can feel compassion for aging, and we can feel compassion for a hurt animal. We stop. We offer time, love, money, and support. But in order to do this, we must feel. There are moments when we cannot, and it would hurt us too much to feel the pain of the room. However, we must be aware of that becoming a pattern of fear. We must develop breath and courage and stamina to be with suffering without letting it overtake us.

What if this is an essential part of our spiritual practice at this time? Training to give us the chops to stop and support other beings, to look beyond our own family unit and self and see the whole world as our family? It would be the healing of the colonizer; it would be a deep return to something we have forgotten: that our lives are intertwined, we are on borrowed time, and each action we take impacts this world. Do we choose the self again and again and again? Do we choose spirituality for personal gain? Or do we give love and compassion and generosity as the mystics and saints did? We don't discriminate who we love. We discern who gets close, yes. But we love big and open. What if we taught our kids to do the same? To give more, to share, to pick up trash, to see the whole world as our responsibility together? Imagine the kind of world those acts of love would create.

Dare
to
Feel

REFLECTIONS

- Where and how do you engage with your local community? If this is not something you have practiced, how could you begin? What feelings does this bring up?

- What is your relationship with cultures that are different from yours? If you hold any prejudices, where do they come from, and how does it feel in your body to hold these?

- Is there a way you could reach outside your comfort zone, not to save anyone, but to learn more about your broader community?

- Do you practice random acts of kindness when no one is looking? Without posting or sharing about them? Consider when you have and why.

RITUAL FOR COMMUNITY

Find a friend and make a commitment to do something together for your local community monthly. Perhaps it's hosting a potluck, like Shannon, or donating time at a food bank locally. Perhaps it's a skill swap or clothing exchange. How does it feel in your body to commit to this offering? Make it a ritual by inviting a moment of sacred awareness to whatever you do. Perhaps you say a silent prayer in your heart that your actions multiply. Perhaps it's a gratitude practice before eating at a potluck or asking people to offer any prayers or words before eating.

See this not as something on your to-do list, but as a moment of potential for transforming the heart.

WHY WE CAME

We didn't just come here to chill
and make money
and check things off lists!

We came to wake up!

To stand up!

To blossom!

To heal!

To protect!

To reclaim!

To remember!

TO LOVE!

To be that which
WE ALREADY ARE
underneath thousands of years of human drama,
war,
pain,
fear . . .

A truth awaits us
in our center,
ready to be remembered!

27

Dreaming of a Planet
Where We Dare to Feel

The journey of deep feeling and of walking the transformational path of the heart is complex. The path is mysterious and never-ending. Sometimes we have to deep dive into its caverns and pain in order to find the gold we seek. We must go back and feel the things we couldn't feel then, so that we can love fully now. We cannot love now if our hearts are numb. We cannot love now if we are avoiding the truth of our lives, the most gruesome and painful moments, and the most beautiful ones. The journey of deep feeling is the journey of aliveness. Of the heart reaching out into life and opening up, even when it feels safer to stay closed.

With this book, my hope is that **in daring to feel again—in daring to notice your heart's shadows and turn toward them, in daring to notice how you open and close your heart—that you have increased your capacity for love, and for meeting life's most painful and beautiful moments with the same level of openness and courage.** I hope that, like me, you might come to recognize this as the spiritual path. As the path of living as love. And that you see that the language and currency of this path is feeling. I hope all of this, because in a world where fear abounds, people choosing to walk the path of feeling it all, facing their own heart shadows and closures, and staying open and living from love, are so deeply needed. Because the time is truly now for us to live what we claim to stand for.

Sometimes I sit and wonder what it would be like to live on a planet where love ruled and where we dared to feel it all. In my imagination, this would be a world where people didn't hoard resources and war wasn't a thing, and we didn't suck the lifeblood out of the planet. A place without violence, a place of sharing wealth and resources, of walking outside at night with no fear. Of all children having enough food. This would also be a world where people dared to grieve together. To mourn openly. To cry in public. To feel joy and to laugh loudly when it was time to laugh. To not be afraid of connection and love. And to not be afraid of pain. A world where instead of trying to avoid pain, we knew how to help each other stay open in it. In this world, we collectively know there is more than enough love to go around, more than enough of everything, because we are not lying to ourselves and we are not living from fear.

In a world where feeling was valued alongside doing, things would be slower. There would be less urgency. There would be space to slow down and process life, to be with what we were feeling, instead of rushing to the next thing. In a world where deeply felt lived experiences counted more than fancy degrees, decisions might be made by wise elder councils. Indigenous wisdom honored and prayer treated as daily self-care. In a world where emotions were allowed to be felt, deeply, there would be circles for grieving and raging and laughing and sharing hard stories. This would be a world where we didn't have to hold the burdens of our lineages alone. A place where we were encouraged to seek to heal the things that went on before we came.

Instead of simply locking people away in prisons, we might make circles for them and hold them and love them and pray with them, and they might be helped. Giving a space for all to feel. We would focus on turning the drivers of murder, war, incest, violence, and addiction toward love and healing. Perhaps this sounds a bit "kumbaya" to you. But we must turn toward each of our inner cynics as we ask: Why don't we deserve a world where love rules and not fear?

And this is the world we are weaving, you and I, when we dare to feel the pains of the past, when we allow ourselves to stop and mourn and grieve and share and speak, when we dare to fully feel our joy and pleasure, when we allow it all to keep our hearts open and alive to life.

The world I've described may feel far-fetched, but you are dreaming it into form by healing yourself, by turning toward your own shadows, by cultivating compassion, by choosing to stay open to life, by listening to the stories of those who are hurting and keeping your heart open through it all. By daring to feel the truth of each moment. Daring to notice when you mess up. Daring to stop and apologize. Daring to notice somebody else's pain or need, but not at the expense of your own. Daring to notice the stories of people beyond your family and race and class. You dare to feel every time you dare to listen deeply, letting the stories and words of others open your heart and stir your emotions.

You are saying "yes" to all of this by being here. Thank you—I see you. It might feel hard to feel it all some days, but please don't give up, my dear. **Let your loving and your resting and your daily prayers and rituals and stories all be a return to deep feeling and a return to the heart.** A reminder of the world we are weaving, together, into reality. A world we can choose to be living in right now.

I AM WILLING

I am willing to take the unknown path.
I am willing to stand on the cliff and be the first to jump.
I am willing to sit in the fires of my deepest pains.
I am willing to breathe instead of running away.
I am willing to admit my failings.
I am willing to be the awkward one.
I am willing to look dumb.
I am willing to fall,
to break,
to die,
and be reborn again.
I am willing.

Acknowledgments

Thank you to Mom and Papie for being the best gurus and souls I could have chosen as parents, helping me to learn such deep, beautiful spiritual lessons in this life that I can share with the world. Thank you for letting me share about our lives together, even though I know it is not always easy to have a daughter who is a writer. Thank you for the encouragement you have always bestowed so freely upon me to follow my dreams.

My heart's deepest gratitude to all the friends and lovers who have given me this life with each shared experience and filled each story with rich value and humor and wisdom. You are also my companions on the path, my teachers and greatest loves.

Thank you to Ruby Warrington for being my book doula, dear friend, and writing mentor for a great many years. Deep gratitude beyond words. My writing would not be the same without you. Our collaborations and creative brainstorms are some of my favorite moments in life.

Many thanks to Dr. Jennifer Selig for being such a great memoir writing teacher as I developed many of these stories.

To Diana Ventimiglia at Sounds True, I am so grateful you gave such an enthusiastic blessing for me to have such artistic expression in this book and to tell stories and share poems and let that be of just as much value as linear teaching books. Thank you times a million for letting me be an artist, a poet, a storyteller, and a teacher. And Lyric, Jade, and Evelyn for your amazing editing support, thank you for going on the journey with me.

My profound gratitude to Mesha, for all your deep wisdom and support as I faced my deepest challenges and walked in some dark shadowlands of the heart. Without your loving support, I do not know if I would have had the courage to open my heart past the hurts of my past. Thank you for being such an amazing guide on the path.

And thank you to Eli, who is the gift after all the years of heart healing and shadow facing and deep opening, and prayers and prayers. To receive a love like ours, after all the hard work, is the greatest gift of all.

About the Author

Alexandra is an author, artist, spiritual seeker, and teacher of embodied spirituality and transformation. Her first book, *F*ck Like a Goddess: Heal Yourself, Reclaim Your Voice, Stand in Your Power* debuted in 2020 with Sounds True. It has been published in multiple languages and sold worldwide. She supports thousands of women as a mentor, coach, and teacher, leading retreats and working with women one-on-one in their journeys of healing, embodiment, and spirituality. For more, visit alexandraroxo.com.

About Sounds True

Sounds True was founded in 1985 by Tami Simon with a clear mission: to disseminate spiritual wisdom. Since starting out as a project with one woman and her tape recorder, we have grown into a multimedia publishing company with a catalog of more than 3,000 titles by some of the leading teachers and visionaries of our time, and an ever-expanding family of beloved customers from across the world.

In more than three decades of evolution, Sounds True has maintained our focus on our overriding purpose and mission: to wake up the world. We offer books, audio programs, online learning experiences, and in-person events to support your personal growth and awakening, and to unlock our greatest human capacities to love and serve.

At SoundsTrue.com you'll find a wealth of resources to enrich your journey, including our weekly *Insights at the Edge* podcast, free downloads, and information about our nonprofit Sounds True Foundation, where we strive to remove financial barriers to the materials we publish through scholarships and donations worldwide.

To learn more, please visit SoundsTrue.com/freegifts or call us toll-free at 800.333.9185.

Together, we can wake up the world.

sounds true
WAKING UP THE WORLD